PADDLE LONDON

The Best Places to Go with a Paddleboard, Kayak or Canoe

ADLARD COLES
Bloomsbury Publishing Plc
50 Bedford Square, London, WC1B 3DP, UK
Bloomsbury Publishing Ireland Limited,
29 Earlsfort Terrace, Dublin 2, D02 AY28, Ireland

BLOOMSBURY, ADLARD COLES and the Adlard Coles logo are trademarks of Bloomsbury Publishing Plc

First published in Great Britain 2026
This edition published 2026

Copyright © Anu Aladin, 2026
Map Illustrations © Richard Thomson, 2026

Anu Aladin has asserted her right under the Copyright, Designs and Patents Act, 1988, to be identified as Author of this work

All rights reserved. No part of this publication may be: i) reproduced or transmitted in any form, electronic or mechanical, including photocopying, recording or by means of any information storage or retrieval system without prior permission in writing from the publishers; or ii) used or reproduced in any way for the training, development or operation of artificial intelligence (AI) technologies, including generative AI technologies. The rights holders expressly reserve this publication from the text and data mining exception as per Article 4(3) of the Digital Single Market Directive (EU) 2019/790

A catalogue record for this book is available from the British Library

ISBN: PB: 978-1-3994-1680-1; ePDF: 978-1-3994-1679-5; ePub: 978-1-3994-1677-1

2 4 6 8 10 9 7 5 3 1

Typeset in Frutiger by Rod Teasdale

Printed and bound in China by RR Donnelley Asia Printing Solutions Limited

To find out more about our authors and books visit www.bloomsbury.com and sign up for our newsletters. For product safety related questions contact productsafety@bloomsbury.com

IMPORTANT SAFETY NOTICE AND LEGAL DISCLAIMER

This book contains descriptions of paddling routes and locations around the UK. Undertaking any activity on or near water carries with it some risks that cannot be entirely eliminated, for example, you might get lost on a route or caught in bad weather. The information contained in this book should not be relied upon as a sole means of navigation. Users should consult all other relevant and available publications and information, such as the local Harbour Authority guidance or Waterway Authorities Navigation Notices. Users should also check local weather and water conditions with the appropriate authorities prior to departure. The guidance contained in this book is based on the accumulated experience of the author. Such guidance is generic and takes no account of users' own experience, advice from other paddlers, actual or forecast meteorological conditions, water conditions or other waterway users powered or otherwise.

All internet addresses given in this book were correct at the time of going to press. Bloomsbury Publishing Plc does not have any control over, or responsibility for, any third-party websites referred to or in this book.

The publishers and authors accept no responsibility for any errors or omissions, or for any accident, loss or damage arising from the misuse of information or guidance contained in this book.

PADDLE LONDON

The Best Places to Go with a Paddleboard, Kayak or Canoe

ANU ALADIN

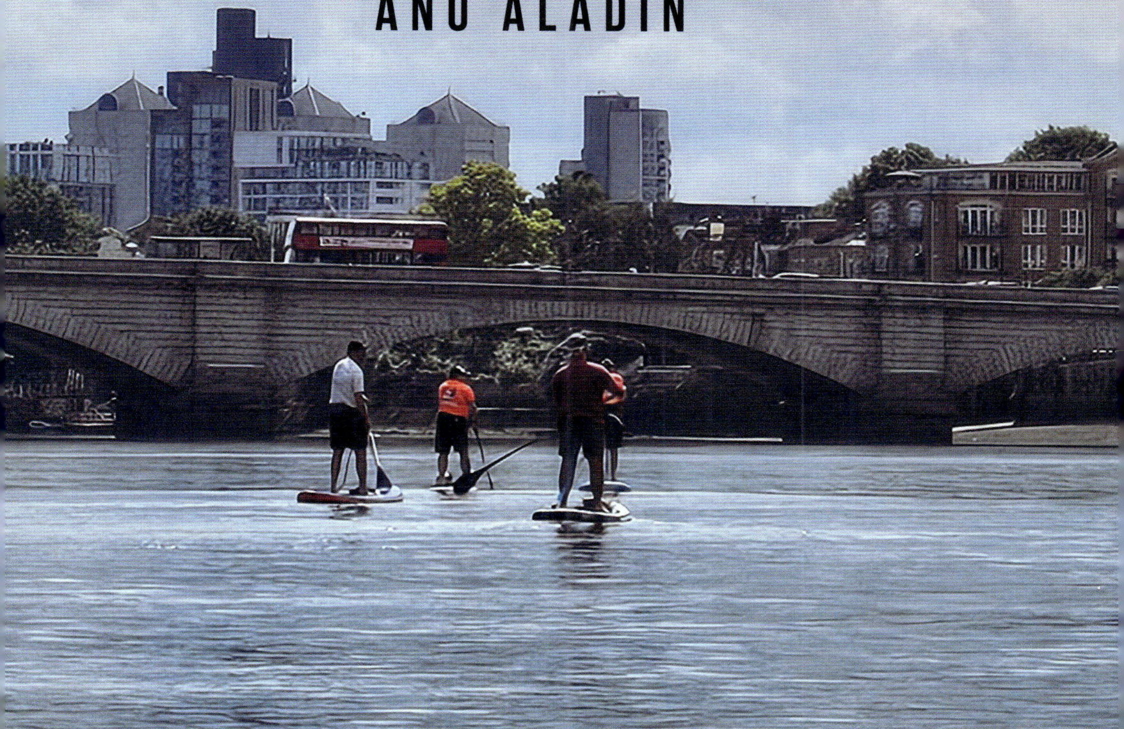

ADLARD COLES

LONDON · OXFORD · NEW YORK · NEW DELHI · SYDNEY

CONTENTS

Introduction	6
Using this book	8
Safety	10

RIVER THAMES — 16

01	Reading to Wargrave via St Patrick's Stream	20
02	Maidenhead to Hedsor Water	26
03	Windsor and Backwaters	30
04	Windsor to Hampton Court	34
05	Weybridge	40
06	Hampton to Molesey and Thames Aits	46
07	Thames Ditton to River Ember	52
08	Kingston to Hampton Court	58
09	Kingston to Teddington	63
10	Ham House to Teddington Lock	67
11	Richmond to Eel Pie Island	71
12	Kew Bridge to Richmond	75
13	Putney to Kew Bridge	80
14	Chelsea to Kew	84
15	Battersea to Greenwich	89

CANALS — 96

16	Rickmansworth to Watford (Grand Union)	98
17	Rickmansworth to Uxbridge (Grand Union)	102
18	West Drayton to Slough (Grand Union)	106
19	Hayes to Hanwell (Grand Union)	110
20	Brentford to Fox Inn at Hanwell (Grand Union/River Brent)	115
21	Hayes to Greenford (Grand Union)	120

22 Greenford to Harlesden (Grand Union)	124
23 Little Venice to Kensal Green (Grand Union)	128
24 Camden to Maida Hill Tunnel (Regent's)	133
25 Camden to King's Cross (Regent's)	138
26 Islington to Hackney (Regent's)	142
27 Hackney to Mile End (Regent's)	146
28 London Legacy Loop (Limehouse Basin)	150
29 Limehouse Loop (Lee Navigation)	154
30 Hertford to Broxbourne (Lee Navigation)	158
31 Broxbourne to Ponders End (Lee Navigation)	162
32 Ponders End to Tottenham Hale (Lee Navigation)	166
33 Clapton to Hackney Wick (Lee Navigation)	170

OTHER WATERWAYS 174

34 Crookham Wharf to Colt Hill (Basingstoke)	176
35 Colt Hill to Greywell Tunnel (Basingstoke)	180
36 Godalming to Shepperton (Wey Navigations)	184
37 Marsh Lane to Manor Farm (Jubilee River)	189
38 Esher to Hersham (River Mole)	193
39 West Reservoir Centre (Stoke Newington)	196
40 Royal Victoria Dock (Docklands)	200

Beyond the Paddle	204
Acknowledgements	206
Photo credits	206
Index	207

KEY TO DIFFICULTY

💧 Suitable for all, especially beginners
💧💧 Intermediate paddles, some experience/knowledge necessary
💧💧💧 For experienced paddlers only
💧💧💧💧 More challenging paddles

INTRODUCTION

I still remember the uncontrollably shaking legs I had on my first ever paddleboarding experience, a beginner's lesson on holiday in Falmouth in 2011. It was hardly the effortless glide I had admired a year earlier in Hawaii, where I saw a paddleboarder moving across the water with such grace that it sparked my curiosity. Yet, despite my wobbles, there was something about SUP that hooked me. Maybe it was the Blue Mind state, the deep sense of calm that comes with being on the water. Or perhaps it was that paddleboarding got me out of the fast lane and demanded my full attention, keeping me present in a way I had always struggled with. Standing on the board made me feel independent and free.

How do you even paddle in London? No turquoise waters of Hawaii or Cornwall here. I joined a local club. I may have cried on my first Guy Fawkes paddle on the tidal Thames. I had stopped to take a photo of the fireworks up above, only to realise I had drifted far from the group with the strong flow. Back then, I knew nothing about tides. But I kept going. I bought my first inflatable SUP in 2013. In a moment of madness, I trained as a SUP instructor. London may not seem like the obvious watersports destination, but for quite a few years I found myself teaching others to paddle on London's canals and the Thames.

I live in a one-bed flat in Richmond, without a car, which is not the typical set-up for a paddleboarder. But paddling isn't just

ABOVE Regent's Canal runs through the leafy Primrose Hill.

LEFT The peaceful side of Camden, best seen from the water.

RIGHT Seeing London from a whole new perspective.

INTRODUCTION

ABOVE Plenty of waterside pubs waiting to be discovered.

ABOVE Love it or not, portaging is part of paddling adventures.

for van owners or coastal getaways. You don't always have to go far for adventure.

I hope this book inspires you to explore Greater London's waterways year-round by paddle power. The Thames ebbs and flows through the capital, passing centuries of history, while canals, reservoirs and docks offer calm, sheltered routes. Wilderness is closer than you think. Along the way, with this slow pace of travelling, you absorb your surroundings and find hidden pockets of nature, architecture, culture and art. You get acquainted with London from a whole new angle.

Be warned, you may just fall in love with urban paddling. Paddle in London, paddle for life.

USING THIS BOOK

London's blue spaces are made for exploring, whether you're a visitor or a tourist in your own city. The 40 routes in this book are all within an hour of London, from short paddles to full-day adventures. Some are suitable for beginners, others for more experienced paddlers. Routes can also be linked for longer trips.

Lowdown Each route starts with a quick summary to help you plan.

Difficulty rating Paddling environments are rated based on normal conditions for wind, flow, water levels and tides. What feels easy quickly becomes more challenging if natural forces intensify. Consider these ratings a guideline – only you know your ability.

- ♦ Easy – Canals, reservoirs and docks with little to no current
- ♦♦ Moderate – Similar but with potential hazards like current, weirs and traffic. Rivers and river navigations
- ♦♦♦ Difficult – Faster-flowing rivers, tidal rivers
- ♦♦♦♦ Advanced – Fast tidal rivers with heavy traffic and obstacles

Launch, exit, distance and portages Launch and exit details help you evaluate accessibility. Distance and number of portages give an idea of the effort required, while lock names help track progress along the route.

Licence In England, most non-tidal inland waterways require a licence. Think of it as a way to support the care and upkeep of the water network. Licence checks are becoming more common.

The most comprehensive licence option is a Paddle UK 'On the Water' membership (paddleuk.org.uk), which gives you access to 4,500km of waterways in England and Wales. It covers all licensed routes in this book and includes public liability insurance. Membership starts at £60 a year for new members.

If you don't have this membership, you'll need to buy separate licences for each waterway from the relevant navigation authority. Details are listed under each route or section.

Start and finish What3Words is used to reference the start and finish locations, also shown on the maps. Get the app at what3words.com. Both public transport and driving details are provided, with estimated walking times to help you plan how far you'll need to carry your kit.

Public transport London's transport network makes it easy to reach the waterways. As an urban adventurer, you've got plenty of options: Underground (Tube), buses, Docklands Light Railway (DLR), Overground, Elizabeth Line, river services, cable car and National Rail. Contactless tap-in, tap-out is the easiest way to pay, with daily and weekly fare caps. For National Rail, off-peak returns and railcards offer savings. For last-mile transport, taxis, Uber and Bolt are useful. Buses aren't listed individually, but they're everywhere. Plan ahead at tfl.gov.uk and always check for disruptions. London's transport loves a weekend surprise.

USING THIS BOOK   9

ABOVE Pack wisely for one-way paddles.

Driving
For inner London routes, driving is not advised. But for select spots further out, a car can be practical. Share lifts if possible and keep in mind:

- Parking – Street parking is often limited to two hours. Always check signage and don't leave valuables in the car.
- Car parks – Few launch spots have dedicated parking, but nearby options are listed. Parking is usually charged, with height restrictions and free options noted. Check ahead, as rules may change. Walking time to the launch spot is included, but electric car charging availability should be confirmed separately.
- ULEZ and Congestion Charge – Charges apply in Central London and some surrounding areas. Details at tfl.gov.uk.
- Parking apps – Apps like RingGo, Parkopedia and JustPark help to find, book and pay for parking.
- Shuttle system – If paddling with a friend, consider a shuttle for one-way routes: leave one car at the start and another at the end.

Paddle providers
Local paddle providers have been included. Most listed providers are for paddleboarding, as kayaking and canoeing often have well-established club systems. SUP, by contrast, is a newer sport where many start by simply buying a board and heading out on their own. Connecting with local providers can be a great way to meet fellow paddlers, who love showing off their area.

SAFETY

Planning There is an element of risk in paddling, but good planning makes the activity both safer and more enjoyable. Complete your own risk assessment, stay flexible and be ready to drop your plans if conditions are not right. Refer to Paddle UK's Paddlesafer guidance (paddleuk.org.uk).

The most important safety rule? Know your limits and pick routes that match your skills. Make sure you can self-rescue before heading out. If you are unsure, take a lesson – paddle providers are listed throughout the book. Keep learning and connect with local clubs. Paddling with others, especially those with more experience, is the best way to level up your paddling game.

Things to check:

- Weather and water conditions – Check the forecast, wind – both steady and gusts, flow rate, tides and water levels. Check again before launching and keep

PADDLE UK AND SUP SAFETY

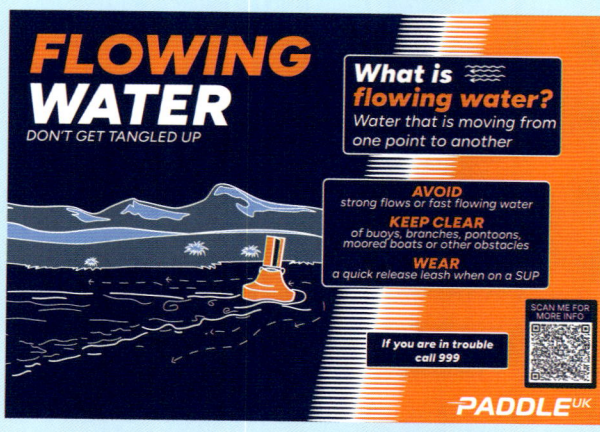

Paddle UK offers this insight into the organisation's role and commitment to safety:

Paddle UK is the national governing body for paddlesports and is a membership organisation. It provides waterways licences for members, granting access to over 4,500km of waterways. Paddle UK actively campaigns for access and clean blue spaces, offers insurance benefits, and provides access to high quality guidance and advice for paddlers.

SUP Safety:

Stand Up Paddleboarding is a fantastic activity with numerous benefits for both your physical and mental

SAFETY

- monitoring while on the water.
- Waterway rules – Know the relevant authority and follow their guidance.
- Equipment – Use suitable paddle equipment for the intended route and conditions. Make sure everything is in working order.
- Clothing – Think water temperature, not just air. In London, water is coldest in February, and cold-water shock is real.
- Buoyancy aid/PFD – Always wear one, even if you are a competent swimmer.
- SUP leash – Use the correct type for your environment.
- Phone – Carry a fully charged mobile in a waterproof case. Your phone may be waterproof but it doesn't float.
- Paddle plan – Let someone know where you're going.
- Food and drink – Stay fuelled. Bring water and snacks. In winter, pack a hot drink.

skills. Make sure you can self-rescue before heading out. If you are unsure, take a lesson – paddle providers are listed throughout the book. Keep learning and connect with local clubs. Paddling with experienced paddlers, on routes to match your ability, is a good way to level up your paddling game.

We always emphasise the following key safety points:
- Always wear a buoyancy aid.
- Tell someone where you are going.
- Carry a mobile phone.
- Check the weather.
- Know your limits.

These graphics created by Paddle UK are a useful summary of the key safety considerations:

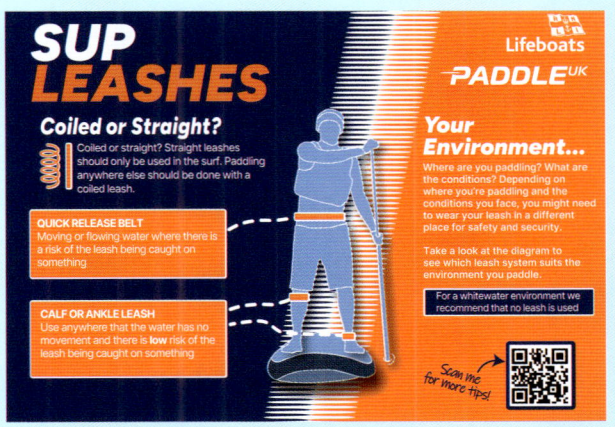

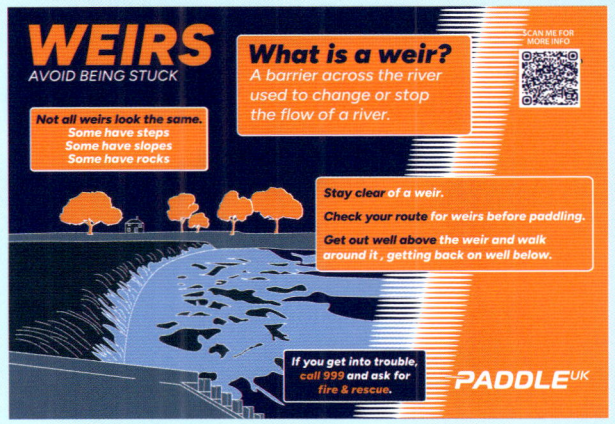

SUP kit

Inflatable boards have revolutionised access to urban paddling. No longer do you need a car, roof rack and storage, just a board on your back and a contactless card in your pocket. There's ample advice out there on choosing an inflatable – check Go Paddling (gopaddling.info), for example. An all-round board is a solid choice, but for urban SUP it is worth considering a touring board. With a pointed nose and a longer, narrower shape, it offers better glide, tracking and speed. You'll quickly grow into it.

Look for a board with a universal fin box so you can swap fins. When inflating, always aim for the recommended maximum PSI. An under-inflated board is more unstable – no one wants to paddle a banana. If pumping by hand feels like a workout instead of a warm-up, invest in a small rechargeable electric pump. Worth every penny.

Your board bag matters too, especially if you are using public transport on a regular basis. Wheels are great for longer walks, but backpack straps are key for stations with stairs. Make sure there is space for your paddle, pump, leash, fin, PFD and any extras. A three-piece paddle is best and not likely to jab a stranger on the Tube.

SUP Leashes

A leash is an essential piece of safety equipment but be sure to choose the right type for where you are paddling. Check the latest guidance at Paddle UK (paddleuk.org.uk).

For flat water routes, a coiled leash is best. It won't drag in the water or catch on obstacles. These usually attach at the ankle or calf and are safe to use where there is no risk of entrapment, such as paddling on canals and reservoirs. On moving water, like the river, stream and river navigation routes featured in this book, add a quick-release (QR) waist belt that attaches to your coiled leash cuff. This set-up lets you detach from your board should the leash or board get caught on something. Just pull the toggle on the belt to release. Practise at home so it feels familiar if you ever need to use it.

Personal flotation devices

In SUP, your board is your main flotation, but Paddle UK also recommend wearing a personal flotation device (PFD). Unlike full life jackets, buoyancy aids help you float but don't fully support you in the water. Fit matters: snug, comfortable and with straps tightened so it stays put if you were to fall in. Waist belt PFDs give more freedom of movement but must be activated manually.

What to wear

Dress for the water, not just the weather. Think: what if I fall in while out there? Because one day you will. It is always a bit of a shock and not necessarily down to you either. Wear quick-drying layers and avoid cotton or denim, which stay wet and cold. Pack spare layers and waterproofs in a dry bag.

In warmer months, active wear works fine. Barefoot paddling is great, but footwear is smart, especially if launching from the water or portaging. If you don't have wet shoes, an old pair of flat trainers or sandals do the job. Sunglasses? Use a strap or say goodbye.

In colder months, hypothermia is a real risk. Dress to stay warm, dry and safe. Wear thermals and add thin layers as needed. For city paddles, neoprene leggings or a Long John/Jane wetsuit with a waterproof top is usually enough. On more remote routes, where getting warm again is harder, a drysuit is worth considering. Sure, it is an investment, but designed to keep you fully dry upon immersion. Full wetsuits can be restrictive, and they are only warm when wet.

Finally, extremities. Freezing feet end fun fast. Proper neoprene boots or sailing boots with waterproof socks are a game-changer. Add gloves and a warm hat and you're good to go.

SAFETY

A Inflatable board
B Water bottle and Thermos
C First aid kit
D GoPro in a floating case
E Dry bag
F Sweets
G Hat
H Pump
I Board bag
J PFD
K Dry bag for board bag, pump and kit

Responsible paddling

The health of London's blue spaces depends on how we treat them. Take everything with you, pick up litter and keep noise to a minimum. And yes, there is more to London's wildlife than the usual city dwellers like rats, pigeons and foxes. Be mindful of all urban nature, especially during breeding seasons. To prevent spread of invasive, non-native species between paddle spots, always check, clean and dry your kit after each outing. For more tips, check the Paddlers' Code (paddlerscode.info).

Navigation

When paddling on urban waterways, stay aware and follow local rules. The 'rules of the road' are the opposite to those on land. On the water, all craft are required to keep to the right whenever possible. Always give way to powered craft – they are bigger, slower to manoeuvre and may not see you. A 30-tonne vessel is not something you want to challenge. Respect anglers and moored boats.

Many routes in this book include locks and weirs. Always portage at locks. Weirs control water flow and can be unpredictable – stay well clear of them.

Water quality

Water quality can vary depending on weather conditions. After heavy rainfall, there may be discharges from combined sewer overflows, while dry spells can lead to stagnant water. For an informed decision, check Thames Water's EDM Mapping service (thameswater.co.uk/edm-map). The Thames Tideway Tunnel, a 25km super sewer, was connected in 2025. It is expected to stop 95 per cent of overflow spills into the tidal Thames.

Weil's disease is rare, but to reduce the risk of waterborne infections, cover any cuts, wash hands or use hand sanitiser, shower and clean your kit after use.

Winter paddling

You can paddle all year round in London. Check conditions with the navigation authority, especially on rivers, where strong flows and rising water levels are more common. Canals, reservoirs and docks are safer alternatives. Bundle up and enjoy the winter magic.

Toilets

Public toilets are scarce and bushes are often not an option. Ask local businesses to use their loos but it is polite to buy something in return. A Canal & River Trust key can be purchased online for under £5. It unlocks toilets and other facilities along the network, definitely worth keeping on your key chain.

Pack smart

One-way routes are an ideal way to explore, but carrying all your kit means you have to pack smartly. A few tips to make life easier:

- Dry bag hack – A 60-litre tube-shaped dry bag is a top pick. Most SUP wheelie bags fit inside if rolled tightly and strapped. A pump, too. Share a pump with others to cut down on bulk. Carrying one big item when portaging is much easier than juggling multiple pieces with your board and paddle.
- Bag-in-a-bag approach – Keep essentials in a separate small dry bag and use additional lightweight roll-closure dry bags like compression sacks for things like waterproofs.
- Dress for the paddle – Travel in your paddle clothes and shoes. It is London. No one cares.
- Dry bag extras – Duct tape (for repairs), hand sanitiser, an emergency foil blanket (winter paddling essential), karabiners, high-calorie snacks and some cash for emergencies.

SAFETY 15

ABOVE Street art speaks boldly.

RIVER THAMES

Say 'Thames' and most people picture the river flowing past Big Ben, the London Eye and Tower Bridge. But paddle it and you discover a river that is much more than just a scenic backdrop.

The Thames is England's longest river, rising in Gloucestershire and meandering through several counties into London and the Thames Estuary before meeting the North Sea. The Thames is fed by a network of tributaries, some visible, others underground, gathering strength as it travels downstream.

The 15 routes in this book take you through different stretches of the river, from the rural, non-tidal Lower Thames to the tidal, urban waterway in the heart of London. Escape to tranquil backwaters, paddle past historic sites, under picturesque bridges and, like it or not, portage quite a few locks. Spot birds of prey soaring overhead, chat with random people and find your favourite riverside pub along the way.

The closer to London you get, the more built up the environment. Residential London offers it all – houseboats, houses and high-rises. There is also the working river, with industry, commercial traffic, boatyards and creatives. London depends on the Thames as a major water source.

ABOVE Final stretch on the Thames before arriving in Wargrave.

ABOVE Early start to beat the rowers.

Below Teddington Lock, the Thames becomes tidal. Twice a day, the sea reaches up to Teddington, with a tidal range of 7m. Expect to learn a thing or two about working the slacks, fluvial flow, Thames tides and why Richmond's tides behave so oddly.

Connect with nature that exists alongside people in London. Chance upon a seal – maybe even a harbour porpoise. Fish seek refuge in back channels, while the Thames' signature brown water plays its part in the river's ecosystem. And if you spot a bale of hay hanging from a bridge? That is a story in itself.

Paddling the Thames offers an up-close view of its history, nature and constant movement. It is a river best experienced from the water. Enjoy the adventure.

Planning

Conditions on the Thames endlessly change due to weather, tide, flow, water levels, wind, traffic and events. Plan ahead, check forecasts and river flow before setting out and stay alert on the water.

River flow rate

River flow rate is measured in units of cubic metres per second, usually abbreviated as cumecs. Flow rates are recorded by automatic gauges and published every 15 minutes. Familiarise yourself with what flow rates mean for paddling on specific sections of the river. Local clubs are happy to help.

    GaugeMap – gaugemap.co.uk

    RiverApp – mobile app with handy custom alerts

NON-TIDAL THAMES (ABOVE TEDDINGTON LOCK)

Waterway authority: Environment Agency (EA)

ABOVE Windsor Castle, seen from the river.

The Environment Agency publishes information about river conditions, updated once a day by 11am. The warnings are also displayed at each lock:

- Red boards – Strong stream warning; all boats advised not to navigate.
- Yellow boards – Stream increasing/decreasing; unpowered boats advised not to navigate.

Website: gov.uk/guidance/river-thames-current-river-conditions

Sign up to flood alerts

TIDAL THAMES (BELOW TEDDINGTON LOCK)

Waterway authority: Port of London Authority (PLA)

The best resource for up-to-date information about paddling on the tidal Thames is the PLA's 'Tideway Code: A Code of Practice for rowing and paddling on the Tidal Thames'. Paddling is restricted below Putney Bridge due to heavy traffic and fast flow. Check the requirements and conditions in the Tideway Code.

Tideway Code – pla.co.uk

PLA app for tide data, notices to mariners, events calendar and ebb tide flag warning

LEFT A winter paddle on the Tideway, with Kew Bridge and Brentford ahead.

Tides

The Thames is tidal up to Teddington. Understanding tides is essential for planning any paddle below Teddington Lock. There are two high tides and two low tides each day, with a tidal range of 7m. Flows can exceed 4 knots (7.4km/h).

Above Putney, the incoming flood tide takes about 4.5 hours, while the outgoing ebb tide lasts around 8.5 hours. The tide turns first downstream.

Always check the predicted tide times and heights. Most free tide apps provide forecasts for the next seven days. For long-term planning, the PLA publishes annual tide tables.

>PLA Tide Tables – pla.co.uk

Ebb tide flag warning system

The PLA issues daily ebb tide warnings for the Tideway above Putney Bridge. When the outgoing ebb tide combines with high fluvial flow – the volume of water moving downstream from the non-tidal Thames – it can create dangerous conditions.

- Red flag – Very strong flow: do not go out.
- Yellow flag – Strong flow: caution for beginners or those unfamiliar with the Tideway.
- Green flag – Average conditions.
- Black flag – Low flow: expect lower-than-predicted tides at low water.

>PLA app

In addition, always check the actual river flow rates and assess against your own paddling ability. What is considered a normal range may still be too strong for safe paddling.

Richmond Lock & Weir

Richmond Lock & Weir is a half-tide lock. At half-tide time, the weir sluice gates are lowered into the river to maintain water level at a navigable depth up to Teddington. This means a portage for paddlers. For about two hours around either side of high water, depending on fluvial flows, the weir sluice gates are lifted and you can paddle right through.

Once a year, for about four weeks in October–November, there is a draw-off and the weir is left open for maintenance. This means that the river drains to its natural levels.

Thames Barrier

The Thames Barrier, operated by the EA, is a movable flood barrier that protects London from flooding from the sea. When it is closed, the lack of tidal flow changes river dynamics. Monthly maintenance and test closures are published online.

01 READING TO WARGRAVE VIA ST PATRICK'S STREAM

Yes, it's Berkshire, but don't let that stop you. Reading is under an hour from Central London on the Elizabeth Line, less than half an hour on the fast train, and offers more than just business parks. This 11km downstream paddle takes you through two lock portages, past the pretty village of Sonning and into the backwaters of St Patrick's Stream and the River Loddon, finishing at a riverside pub in Wargrave. A delicious slice of Thames life.

The Lowdown

DIFFICULTY 💧💧

WATER TYPE RIVER

LAUNCH/EXIT Towpath

DISTANCE 9–11km (one way)

PORTAGES 2 (Caversham Lock, Sonning Lock)

LICENCE REQUIRED? Yes

START
- ///attend.round.bikes (1)
- ///pits.drop.status (2)
- Reading (1) (Elizabeth Line, National Rail) – 10 min walk
- Thames Valley Park and Ride (2), Thames Valley Park Dr, Earley, Reading RG6 1PT – 5-min walk

FINISH
- ///exposing.roadways.potato
- Wargrave (National Rail) – 15 min walk
- School Lane Car Park, School Lane, Wargrave RG10 9AA – 10-min walk

A brief history

The Thames is home to many historic bridges, each built for a purpose, connecting communities, boosting trade, asserting power, collecting tolls. Sonning Bridge, built in 1775, is a strong contender for one of the most picturesque. This red-brick arch bridge replaced an earlier wooden structure and remains the only road crossing between Reading

RIGHT Gliding past Sonning. Pretty as a postcard.

RIVER THAMES

ABOVE Riverside property tour.

and Henley. Recently, it has gained fame as an unexpected art gallery. Mysterious installations, accessible only from the water, have appeared on its buttress, including a cashpoint, urinal and letterbox. The Royal Mail even had to clarify that it was 'certainly not an operational posting facility'. Who knows what might pop up next?

The paddle

Reading is at the western end of the Elizabeth Line. Host to Reading Festival, it sits on both the Thames and Kennet rivers.

Start your paddle just a 10-minute walk from Reading station. Cross Vastern Road, follow Lynmouth Road and set up opposite Fry's Island. Along the way, are you able to pass by Fanny's Antiques without peeking inside?

Launch downstream towards the rather elegant Christchurch footbridge. Stay on the right after Reading Bridge to approach the first portage at Caversham Lock. Hidden in the greenery is Thames Lido, a restored Edwardian bathhouse.

After portaging, follow the meandering river between Kings Meadow, Coal Woodland and View and Heron Islands. View Island is home to a hydroelectric plant

LEFT So much going on with this boat moored downstream of Reading.

BELOW River views with character, from grand estates to cosy cottages.

with two Archimedes screws at the weir, generating green energy for Thames Lido. Run by volunteers, a brilliant community effort.

The wide straight ahead is Dreadnought Reach, but first, last call for supplies at Tesco Extra. Their mooring is located just before the River Kennet joins the Thames, flowing in from the right, under Horseshoe Bridge. The opening on the opposite side leads to the aptly named Thames & Kennet Marina.

Those who join the paddle from the Thames Valley Park can put in along the Thames Path, between the rowing club and the Wokingham Waterside Centre. Paddle downstream beside the TVP. Not your average business campus, it is set in 32 hectares of green space, far removed

from its coal power station days. Caversham Lakes are hidden to the north. They were formed through gravel extraction. For any rowing fans, Team GB train at the Redgrave-Pinsent Rowing Lake here.

Sonning Lock is up next. Again, stay right to avoid the weir. The portage is well signposted and it is worth stopping to use the facilities beside the lock keeper's beautifully tended gardens. In summer, the scene comes alive: boats queuing, lively chatter and colourful flowers. Like a storybook.

Soon, you can make out the tower of St Andrew's Church and the quaint village of Sonning on the right. But first, Sonning Bridge. Try to count the 11 arches to the bridge while taking a spin to see if any new art installations have appeared on it. Just past the bridge, the lawn with deckchairs belongs to The Great House. If you fancy a posh stop, this former Elizabethan coaching inn with the original Coppa Club restaurant is ideal. Sonning Boats & Launches does private charter from here. You are at the halfway point of the route.

ABOVE A weathered sign marks the entrance to St Patrick's Stream.

BELOW Always a warm welcome at Sonning Lock.

Below Sonning, the river is wide, dotted with the occasional liveaboard boat. Around the 7km mark, watch for the entrance to St Patrick's Stream. It is easily missed, just a weathered Environment Agency sign declaring it 'Unsuitable for navigation by launches'. Open to paddled craft, this narrow, fast-flowing channel promises an adventurous 3km detour. It saves you from portaging at Shiplake Lock.

After the first bridge, stay left for a fun little chute. Then, just go with the flow, steering through the jungle-like route with overhanging trees, fishing platforms and gentle turns. The water is clear, fish darting below. Spot any kingfishers? After the second bridge, keep right to stay on St Patrick's Stream. Soon, the stream merges with the wider, deeper River Loddon, flanked by riverside homes any estate agent would dream of listing and gardens fit for Chelsea Flower Show.

Turn right at the junction with the Thames, downstream of Shiplake Lock. Boat lovers, take the diversion through John Bushnell Marina. Paddle under the railway bridge and along the river's curve by Wargrave village to reach the St George and Dragon pub. It is the perfect endpoint for food, drinks or a picnic by the riverside tables. Do not miss the fish and chips.

Wildlife highlight — White water lily

(*Nymphaea alba*) Common along the river's edges on this section, admire the white blooms of the alba water lily floating on the surface between June and August. Despite its name, the water lily is not actually a lily but belongs to a different plant family. This hardy native aquatic plant offers shade for fish and a habitat for insects. Its yellow cousin, *Nuphar lutea*, is also widespread in these waters.

ABOVE Quietly drifting through greenery and serenity on St Patrick's Stream.

Tuck in
- Pack your own snacks and drinks or grab some in Reading.
- Along the route, options are limited to the upmarket Coppa Club in Sonning and the St George & Dragon in Wargrave at the finish.

Paddle providers
- Wokingham Waterside Centre – wokinghamwatersidecentre.com
- The SUP Life – thesuplife.co.uk
- Wargrave Boating Club – wargraveboatingclub.co.uk

NEED TO KNOW

■ The non-tidal Thames is managed by the Environment Agency (EA). Paddle craft must be registered with the EA or covered by Paddle UK's 'On The Water' membership.

■ Check river conditions before getting on the water – gov.uk/guidance/river-thames-current-river-conditions.

■ If driving, be aware of Parkrun at Thames Valley Park on Saturday mornings.

■ St Patrick's Stream runs fast all year and is not suitable for beginners.

■ Watch out for anglers in the narrow sections of St Patrick's Stream.

02 MAIDENHEAD TO HEDSOR WATER

Often overlooked next to Windsor, Maidenhead holds its own on the Thames. Start at Boulters Island with riverside parking. Paddle through Cliveden Reach, the stunning stretch that inspired 'The Wind in the Willows', with its wooded banks, small islands and the iconic Cliveden House. Finish with a detour into Hedsor Water, a backwater only accessible by unpowered craft. A non-tidal stretch with a fascinating past, but mainly this 8km lock-free round trip is ideal for soaking up the beauty of the Thames.

The Lowdown

DIFFICULTY

WATER TYPE River

LAUNCH/EXIT Towpath

DISTANCE 8km (return)

PORTAGES 0

LICENCE REQUIRED? Yes

START/FINISH
- ///keen.neck.unfair
- Maidenhead (Elizabeth Line, National Rail) – 10 min taxi
- Boulters Lock Car Park, 7–15 Lower Cookham Rd, Maidenhead SL6 8JN, height restriction 1.9m

ABOVE Exploring the calm, rural beauty of the Thames around Maidenhead.

A brief history

This section of the Thames has long been a popular spot for pleasure craft. Going up the river became a much-loved pastime in the Victorian era, as London grew into the world's largest city. People were drawn to the river to escape urban life – enjoying picnics, punting, rowing and boating. Cheap railway tickets made it possible to do day trips from London. Regattas and festivals soon turned summer weekends into lively social events, with fashion tips shared in publications like *The Thames Times & Fashionable River Gazette*. By the late Victorian era, Boulters Lock was the Piccadilly Circus of the waterway, attracting Londoners in droves, especially during Ascot week. After all, who doesn't love messing about on the river?

The paddle

Maidenhead, just outside the M25 in the Royal Borough of Windsor & Maidenhead, is located on the non-tidal Thames. A fast train from Paddington gets you there in 20 minutes, or take the Elizabeth Line. If you park at Boulters Lock car park, carefully cross the busy Lower Cookham Road to the Thames Path. In front of you is Boulters Island, created by the lock cut, with the lock itself 200m downstream. Launch upstream to your left.

The first stretch is narrow and sheltered before opening into the main river after the island's northern tip. Navigate on the right but stay clear of the far-right channel downstream. It is the flood-relief channel of Jubilee River (see route 37) that takes overflow from the Thames, running parallel to Windsor. No entry allowed from this end.

You are now on Cliveden Reach, one of the Thames's most iconic stretches. Paddle past the steep wooded hillside on your right, keeping an eye out for Cliveden House rising above the trees. In the 1960s, this grand manor played a starring role in the Profumo Affair, a scandal that toppled the government. These days, Cliveden is a National Trust estate with woodland and formal gardens. Fancy staying the night? Rooms at the country house hotel start at £445 and no, breakfast is not included.

Continue paddling below the lush greenery of Cliveden Estate's 150-hectare

ABOVE Cliveden House, perched above the hills.

ABOVE Paddling offers the perfect view of this stretch of the river.

grounds. There are four islands too, collectively known as Bavin's Gulls or Sloe Grove, Picnic Island leading the way. Look out for a boathouse and riverside cottages, including Spring Cottage, where Queen Victoria frequently enjoyed afternoon tea. The Queen's Steps, built to spare Victoria the indignity of wet feet, are still there as you glide past. In summer, expect plenty of activity on the water, from skippered cruises to hired canoes, with boaters of varying skill levels adding to the mix.

ABOVE The Queen's Steps at Cliveden House.

Next stop is Hedsor Water. Stick to the right on this final upstream leg and avoid the three channels splitting left. The first is the former millstream of Lulle Brook, the second leads to Odney Weir and the third, marked 'Lock', runs to Cookham Lock. Instead, paddle straight under the wooden footbridge to enter the secluded stretch, usually too shallow for powered craft.

Follow the gentle curve of the backwater with the wooded Sashes Island on your left. Once a popular angling spot, access is now restricted. Before Cookham Lock, Hedsor Water was the main navigation route. A footbridge marks the old Hedsor Wharf on your left and at 4km, you have reached the turning point. Do not venture further up due to the weir. Turn here and enjoy the scenery in reverse when paddling back to Boulters Island.

Linking route

- 03 Windsor and Backwaters

Wildlife highlight

Red kite (*Milvus milvus*)
Keep an eye on the skies while paddling around Maidenhead and you are likely to see a red kite. These striking birds of prey, with their reddish-brown plumage, forked

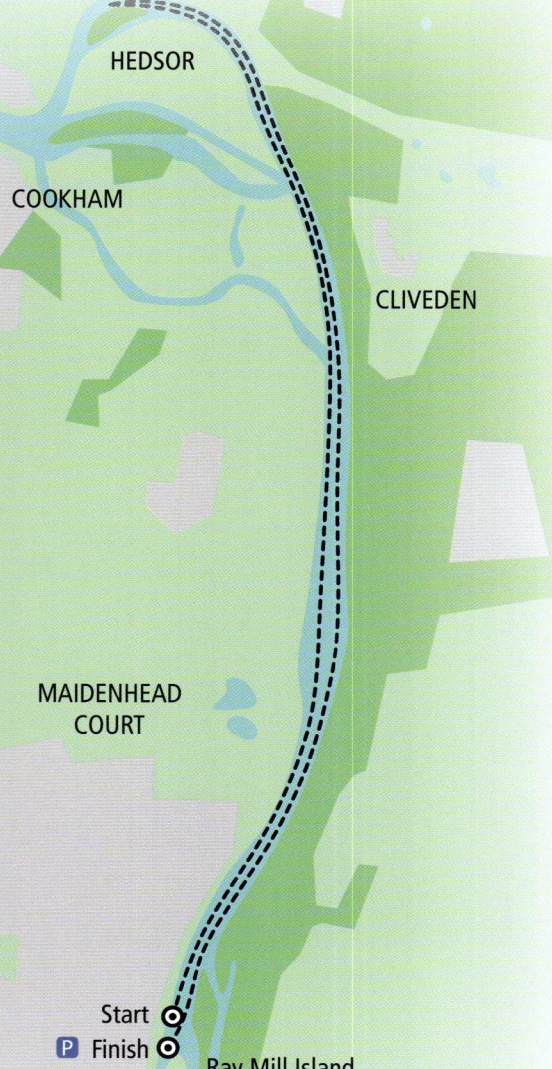

RIVER THAMES

ABOVE A bridge on Hedsor Water.

tails and graceful flight, are a familiar sight here. Once on the brink of disappearing, red kite populations have grown thanks to reintroduction efforts. They are now so common in the area, locals barely notice them. But they are still protected, and worth a moment to appreciate their comeback story.

Tuck in

- Bring your own packed lunch, snacks and drinks.
- The closest option for a bite after the paddle is The Boathouse at Boulters Lock. On the neighbouring Ray Mill Island, there are Island Piazza and the seasonal café.

Paddle providers

- **Paddleboard Maidenhead** – paddleboardmaidenhead.uk
- **AquaPaddle** – aquapaddle.org
- **Boating at Cliveden** – boatingatcliveden.co.uk

NEED TO KNOW

■ The Environment Agency (EA) manages the non-tidal section of the River Thames. Paddle craft must be registered with the EA or you can use Paddle UK's 'On The Water' membership.

■ Before launching, check river conditions – gov.uk/guidance/river-thames-current-river-conditions and navigation updates – gov.uk/guidance/river-thames-restrictions-and-closures.

ABOVE We've got places to be. No stopping.

03 WINDSOR AND BACKWATERS

The River Thames runs through Windsor and Eton and this 8km route lets you explore both from the water. Start with a paddle through serene backwaters, then cruise past the town centre with Windsor Castle as your regal backdrop. Take a detour to see Eton College and Romney Weir, where green energy is produced for the royal family. For best views and some solitude, hit the water early. There is just one lock, but you get to portage it twice.

The Lowdown

DIFFICULTY

WATER TYPE River

LAUNCH/EXIT Towpath

DISTANCE 8km (return)

PORTAGES 1 x 2 (Romney Lock)

LICENCE REQUIRED? Yes

START/FINISH
- ///boil.duty.label
- Windsor & Eton Riverside, Windsor & Eton Central (National Rail) – 10–15-min walk
- Windsor Leisure Centre, Clewer Ave, Stovell Rd, Windsor SL4 5JB – 4-min walk

A brief history

Windsor's name comes from an Anglo-Saxon word meaning 'winding shore', which perfectly describes the town shaped by the Thames. On the opposite bank is Eton. The route passes several historic landmarks, including Windsor Castle, the part-time royal residence of King Charles III, and Eton College, one of Britain's oldest and most prestigious schools. Twenty prime ministers have been educated there.

RIGHT One of the many 'No mooring, no landing' signs.

RIVER THAMES 31

The paddle Windsor draws crowds, so plan ahead. More than 1.5 million people visit the historic town annually. From either train station, it is a 15-minute walk to the launch spot. If driving, park at Windsor Leisure Centre. Kit up on the grassy area by the towpath, just upstream of the railway bridge, across from Baths Island.

Get onto the water and head upstream to your left. Reaching the island's tip, take a sharp right and cross the river. There are two footbridges, paddle under the green one to enter the Cuckoo Weir backwaters. Do not let the name fool you, there are no cuckoos nor a weir, just a swan rescue centre. Follow the stream keeping to the right throughout. It is overgrown and peaceful. Pass under two more bridges, and the third bridge is the exit back onto the main Thames channel.

Take care before crossing the river. The site of the Royal Windsor Racecourse is opposite and the river can be busy with traffic. Watch out for the French Brothers tour boats, which glide by at speed, and the unmistakable yellow amphibious vessels of Windsor Duck Tours. Once clear, cross to the other side and turn left to begin your journey downstream through Windsor.

Stay in the main passage. Beyond the Queen Elizabeth Bridge and Brunel's iron railway bridge, take in the royal view of

LEFT Some portages are well signposted, others leave you to find your own way.

Windsor Castle above. What a treat to paddle in this historic setting. On the left, across Brocas meadows, you may spot Eton College. Boats, tourists and swans abound, the water and Promenade are full of life. Planes to and from Heathrow often soar above as Windsor is on the Heathrow flight path.

Follow the navigation markers at Baths Island, Deadwater Ait and Firework Ait and keep to the right. Windsor Bridge, pedestrians only these days, connects Windsor and Eton. Paddle under it, avoiding the weir on the left, and follow the channel to portage the only lock of the route, Romney Lock (see route 04).

Once back on the water, paddle around the downstream end of Romney Island for a short upstream bonus loop. The paddle perspective provides brilliant views of Eton and its grounds on the right. Up ahead is the weir – stay well clear of it, but do take a moment to check it out. The two leftmost gates have been replaced with twin Archimedes screw turbines, part of a micro-hydropower scheme that provides electricity for Windsor Castle. Sustainable power fit for a king.

Turn around and paddle back. Take the quieter back channel at Deadwater Ait before the railway bridge. Spot the full-size Hawker Hurricane replica on the Promenade side before returning to your starting point.

Linking routes

- 02 Maidenhead to Hedsor Water
- 04 Windsor to Hampton Court

BELOW Eton College is home to 500 years of history and famous alumni.

RIVER THAMES

ABOVE Archimedes screws at Romney Weir.

Wildlife highlight Freshwater fish

The cormorants, herons and anglers around Romney Island are not here for the view. They know they can catch fish like barbel, perch and roach. But with all the obstructions like weirs, sluices and locks along the river, how do fish manage to get around? The answer is a fish pass. Located to the left of the Archimedes screws at Romney Weir, this structure lets fish bypass the weir, making it easier for them to feed and reach their spawning habitats.

Tuck in

- Get supplies or coffee in Windsor before heading out, as there are no riverside venues on this route that are easily accessible from the water.
- For post-paddle, try the Boatman Windsor with its large garden or brave the town centre for more options.

Paddle providers

Canoe & Kayak Adventures – canoeandkayakadventures.co.uk

ABOVE Finding wisdom in canal boat names.

NEED TO KNOW

■ The non-tidal Thames is managed by the Environment Agency (EA). Paddle craft must be registered with the EA or covered by Paddle UK's 'On The Water' membership.

■ Check river conditions before launching – gov.uk/guidance/river-thames-current-river-conditions. Winters especially are often tricky with persistent strong flow that makes paddling dangerous.

04 WINDSOR TO HAMPTON COURT

Palace to Palace is a Thames route like no other. Starting at Windsor Castle and finishing at Hampton Court Palace, the paddle meanders through towns, villages, landmarks and countryside. Grand and sweeping, the Thames offers both wide-open vistas and a changing riverside, from mansions to houseboats, with surprises around every bend. Stop for lunch at a riverside pub before reaching Henry VIII's favourite palace. The stats: 2 palaces, 32km, 8 locks, 36 aits and too many bridges to keep track of.

The Lowdown

DIFFICULTY ●●●

WATER TYPE River

LAUNCH/EXIT Towpath

DISTANCE 32km (one way)

PORTAGES 8 (Locks: Romney, Old Windsor, Bell Weir, Penton Hook, Chertsey, Shepperton, Sunbury, Molesey)

LICENCE REQUIRED? Yes

START
- ///belts.civil.voting
- Windsor & Eton Riverside, Windsor & Eton Central (National Rail) – 10–15-min walk
- Windsor Leisure Centre, Clewer Ave, Stovell Rd, Windsor SL4 5JB – 4-min walk

FINISH
- ///form.aside.views
- Hampton Court (National Rail) – 5-min walk
- Hampton Court Station Car Park, Clewer Ave, Stovell Rd, Windsor SL4 5JB, height restriction 2.08m – 5-min walk

ABOVE Sunbury Lock portage.

RIVER THAMES

A brief history

Royal power has a close connection to the Thames. This route connects two popular palaces.

Windsor Castle was built by William the Conqueror in 1070 and it has been a royal residence since Henry I. Home to 40 monarchs, it is the largest occupied castle in the world, the final resting place of Queen Elizabeth II and a part-time residence for King Charles III, who stays there two days a week.

Hampton Court Palace joined the line of royal residences later. Built in 1515 under the supervision of Cardinal Wolsey, then confiscated and taken over by Henry VIII in 1529, the palace is a mix of architectural styles: Henry expanded it into a Tudor showcase, but William III later enlisted Sir Christopher Wren to update the palace with a more modern, Baroque style.

ABOVE One of the many views of Windsor Castle.

The paddle

The crowds at Windsor train stations are off to Legoland or Windsor Castle. Luckily, you are headed for the river. From the station, it is a 15-minute walk to Windsor Leisure Centre. For those driving, there is a car park, but be prepared for royal rates. Launch downstream from the slipway below the Queen Elizabeth Bridge.

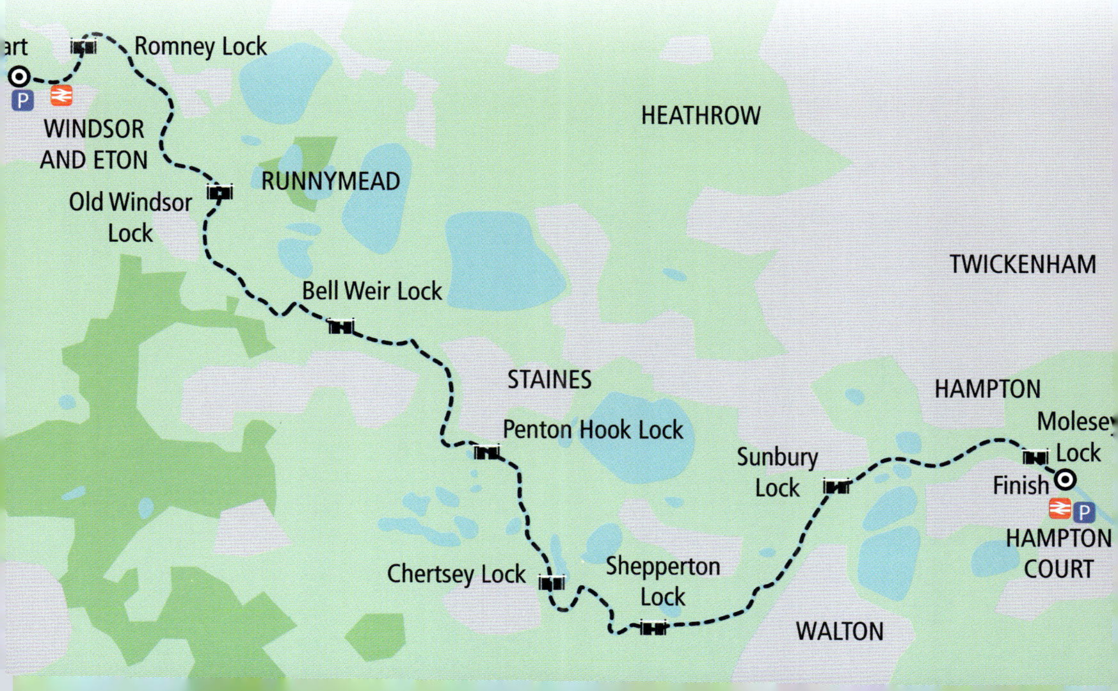

Enter the back channel between the towpath and Baths Island on your right. In Victorian times, this was a swimming area for men and women. Separately, of course. After passing the tip of Deadwater Ait, join the main strait. Watch for swans and river traffic. Tour boats and the yellow

amphibious buses zipping in and out are a regular feature along the Promenade.

The Eton side is lined with the Brocas meadows, but you probably cannot help but focus on Windsor Castle up on its hill. If the Royal Standard is flying atop the round tower, the royals are home. Otherwise, it is the Union flag. After Windsor Bridge, paddle to Romney Lock. Portage here unless the lock keeper invites you in with the boats. How many Le Boat cruisers have you seen already? They are hire boats.

Past Black Potts railway bridge, the flow diverted into the Jubilee (see route 37) in Maidenhead rejoins the Thames. Between Victoria and Albert bridges, enjoy wonderful views of Windsor Home Park and the castle. Do not be tempted to get off the water. The Crown Estate's signs make it clear: no mooring, no landing. Even the Thames Path runs on the opposite side.

The New Cut bypasses the meandering river below Lion Island, leading you straight to Old Windsor Lock. Portage and paddle past Friday and Friary islands to reach Runnymede. Mind the many boat services that operate on this stretch. Paddle by Magna Carta Island in Wraysbury where

ABOVE Floating shelter for the local wildlife.

ABOVE Boatyard and colourful moorings.

RIVER THAMES

LEFT The lush greenery of Windsor Home Park.

RIGHT One of the locks along the Thames route.

BELOW A heron has made this houseboat its home.

in 1215 King John is believed to have reluctantly sealed the historic document. The island's house was on the market for £4.5 million in 2024 – 'a piece of world history', no less.

The riverside National Trust site stretches beneath Cooper's Hill with meadows, memorials and art installations. Worth coming back for a proper wander. At Runnymede Pleasure Grounds, you have reached the 10km mark.

Portage Bell Weir Lock, then paddle under Runnymede Bridge, briefly trading tranquillity for the grumble of the A30 and M25 above. On the left, look out for the replica of the London Stone, a historical marker of the City of London's control over the Thames. Lammas Recreation Ground by Church Island is a good spot for a break, with toilets and a little café.

Onwards to Staines, where the wide river is framed by the three arches of Staines Bridge. Enjoy the riverside harmony: a pub on the right and a church on the left. The River Colne also joins the Thames here.

Three kilometres later, portage at Penton Hook Lock. If it is busy, blame Penton Hook Marina, Britain's largest inland marina, on the right. The scenery shifts as the river winds: green and leafy giving way to more built-up, with houses and boats ranging from grand designs to improvised fixes. Quite a few For Sale signs, too. Waterfront properties are best viewed by paddling.

Paddle under the M3 bridge, then pass Chertsey Bridge with its five arches. Move left to avoid the weir, where the Abbey River joins the Thames. Portage at the lock just beyond and you have arrived at the 20km mark.

The next section is a maze of islands and waterways. Keep left at the first ait, leaving the private residential Pharaoh's Island on your right. Consider a pit stop at the Thames Court pub with a large garden as they serve nice pub classics. If you stop here, the easiest way to portage Shepperton Lock after is to walk past the lock and put in below. Otherwise, keep to the left bank past the top of the weir and follow the portage signs.

Look out for the Shepperton-Weybridge ferry. At the Wey Junction, cross to the right to paddle under D'Oyly Carte Island footbridge. The island has quite the past (see route 05). Stay on the right to navigate Desborough Cut unless you prefer the natural looping course. Both routes take you to Walton Bridge.

Stay on the right to Sunbury Lock Cut. Wheatley's Ait, with a weir at both ends, is part owned by the Environment Agency, part by the residents. Once well past the weirs, portage via the rollers on the left. It is slippery, so step carefully. Re-enter the water from the wooden walkway often frequented by Canada geese.

The final leg is an adventure past another eight islands, reservoirs and plenty of wildlife (see route 06). Stay on the right-hand side of the main channel throughout. Portage at Molesey Lock before arriving in style at Hampton Court Palace. Paddle under Hampton Court Bridge, then take a moment to appreciate the favourite palace of Henry VIII. Lots of activity here, so watch out for tour boats. There are moorings just in front or take out below the bridge on the Hampton Court side (see route 08).

Hampton Court deserves a full day of exploration. Or a week. Perhaps save it for a trip without all your paddle kit.

Linking routes:

- 02 Maidenhead to Hedsor Water
- 03 Windsor and Backwaters
- 05 Weybridge
- 06 Hampton to Molesey and Thames Aits
- 08 Kingston to Hampton Court

ABOVE D'Oyly Carte island.

Wildlife highlight

Egyptian goose (*Alopochen aegyptiaca*) These so-called geese, which are actually ducks, are often seen lounging on the lawns of Windsor Home Park. Waterfowl that prefer dry land. Native to the Nile Valley and once sacred in Egypt, they were introduced to Britain as ornamental birds in the 19th century. Initially, they struggled to adapt but the numbers are now exploding thanks to milder winters. Their most distinctive feature? A brown eye mask that gives them a Cleopatra-like glamour.

Tuck in
Pick up supplies or coffee in Windsor before you hit the water. Along the way, you are not short of riverside stops: Harvester Bells of Ouzeley, Magna Carta tea-room, Runnymede-on-Thames, Little Green Boat Company café, Slug & Lettuce, Swan pub and hotel, Thames Court, Ferry

RIVER THAMES

ABOVE Final stretch toward the finish.

Coffee Shop, D'Oyly's Cafe, The Anglers Walton on Thames, Weir Hotel and Phoenix.
  Near Hampton Court, check out The Mitre and Mezzet Box, both on the water, plus several other places to eat and drink in Molesey, especially on Bridge Road.

NEED TO KNOW

■ The non-tidal Thames is managed by the Environment Agency (EA). Paddle craft must be registered with the EA or covered by Paddle UK's 'On The Water' membership.

■ Check river conditions before launching – gov.uk/guidance/river-thames-current-river-conditions.

Paddle providers

Canoe & Kayak Adventures – canoeandkayakadventures.co.uk
Elmbridge Canoe Club – elmbridgecanoeclub.com
Paddle Up – paddleup.co.uk
Hampton Court Paddle Sports – hamptoncourtpaddlesports.com

BELOW Reaching the grand Hampton Court Palace.

05 WEYBRIDGE

A serene paddle setting in the Surrey town of Weybridge covering three waterways in one trip. This 8.5km return paddle takes you from the Thames to the Wey Navigation and the natural River Wey, offering a slice of country life just 30 minutes from London. Discover private islands with quirky stories, grand mansions, tranquil backwaters, grazing cows and a touch of adventure. Now the secret is out.

A brief history

Not exactly tropical, but there are almost 200 islands on the River Thames. This paddle will get you acquainted with a few of them. There is the private D'Oyly Carte Island, named after the theatre visionary who built a mansion on the island in the 1890s and hosted legendary parties. You can now visit a café on the island. Desborough Island, artificially created in the 1930s to reduce flooding, houses a

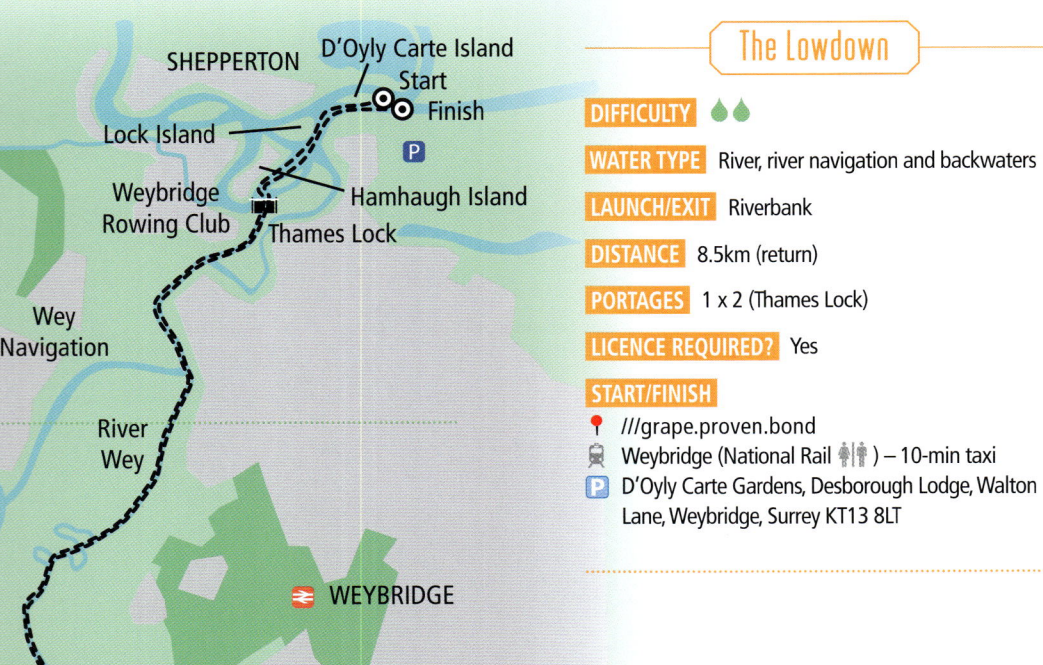

The Lowdown

DIFFICULTY 💧💧

WATER TYPE River, river navigation and backwaters

LAUNCH/EXIT Riverbank

DISTANCE 8.5km (return)

PORTAGES 1 x 2 (Thames Lock)

LICENCE REQUIRED? Yes

START/FINISH
- ///grape.proven.bond
- Weybridge (National Rail 🚻) – 10-min taxi
- D'Oyly Carte Gardens, Desborough Lodge, Walton Lane, Weybridge, Surrey KT13 8LT

RIVER THAMES 41

ABOVE Footbridge to D'Oyly Carte Island leading to the mansion behind.

ABOVE The pet croc is long gone... allegedly.

water treatment facility. Shepperton Lock is managed from Lock Island, while Hamhaugh Island has been transformed from farmland into a private residential hideaway.

Thames Lock is the entrance to the Wey Navigation, one of England's earliest canalised rivers with locks, weirs and cuts. The Navigation turned the meandering River Wey into a key trade route between London and Guilford. Although its founder, Sir Richard Weston, did not live to see its completion in 1653, it helped Surrey become one of the more affluent counties in the country. Today, the National Trust looks after the navigation as a leisure waterway.

The paddle

If you arrive by car, leave it at the riverside car park next to Elmbridge Canoe Club. Launch from the Thames path or, if vacant, use the pontoon in front of the canoe club. The first stretch of water on this route is a picturesque part of the non-tidal Thames.

You are right in front of the mysterious D'Oyly Carte Island, one of the many private Thames islands in the area. Paddle upstream under the narrow metal footbridge that connects the island to the mainland. The mansion on the island is being restored to its former Victorian glory. Let's see if they bring back the pet crocodile. The 'Mind the Croc' sign at their café is just for laughs... isn't it?

Follow the curve of the river left. A pedestrian ferry runs to Shepperton on the opposite bank. There is a spaghetti junction here. Keep both Lock and Hamhaugh islands on your right — they used to be one island. You can hear the soft hum of the nearby weir here. Paddle past the 'Wey Navigation' sign on the left, it only applies to boats. Continue straight along the narrow island in front of the main Whittet's Ait until you reach Weybridge Rowing Club on your left.

Get off at the rowing club's pontoon, making sure not to intrude with their activities. Carry your kit down the right-hand side of the club to the back gate. This is the designated portage for non-powered craft heading through to Thames Lock, the last lock on the Wey Navigation.

The pretty lock keeper's cottage is on the other side. There is no need to walk across the bridge, just keep going right past the lock and look for the steps in front of the National Trust visitor centre to embark your adventure on the Wey Navigation, the second waterway of this route.

The change in mood is evident. The Wey is narrower and more intimate, shaded with greenery all around. It has the character of a backwater even if this section is open to boat traffic. Glide past the elegant homes of Weybridge, with their gardens and private moorings. A scene straight out of 'Country Living'! Follow the gently meandering waterway to the wide wharf pool and Wey Bridge.

Here, the navigation splits from the natural river. The right arch, marked 'Navigation', starts a 32km route with locks up to Godalming (see route 36). Skip that today and take the left channel onto the River Wey flowing towards Brooklands,

Byfleet and beyond. The river portion is open to the elements, with changing conditions like water levels and flow, occasionally fallen trees and thick pockets of floating pennywort.

You are now on the third waterway of the route. Paddle upstream along Wey Meadows,

getting a rare view into some more amazing houses. There is also abundant greenery, sweeping reeds and overhanging trees. You may spot a 'Neighbourhood Watch' sign on an uninhabited island with a congregation of ducks. After the railway bridge, the route becomes even more untamed and tranquil, with only a few pylons as a reminder of urban life.

If conditions allow, venture up to Nine Arches Bridge and continue to Seven Arches Bridge before turning back. Enjoy the return trip, cruising back aided by the gentle flow of the Wey.

TOP LEFT Portage through Weybridge Rowing Club.

BOTTOM LEFT Hidden passages along the River Wey.

TOP Grand homes with enviable river access.

RIGHT Peaceful waters, just you and nature.

ABOVE Nothing beats an evening paddle.

ABOVE RIGHT A midweek escape.

LEFT Lock keeper's cottage at Thames Lock.

BELOW Golden hour on the water.

RIVER THAMES 45

Linking routes
- 04 Windsor to Hampton Court
- 36 Godalming to Shepperton (Wey Navigations)

Wildlife highlight

Floating pennywort (*Hydrocotyle ranunculoides*). Floating pennywort, with its kidney-shaped, glossy leaves, looks lush and green on the water's surface. Originally from South America, it was brought to the UK for garden ponds and it certainly loves the stagnant or slow-moving freshwater habitats of London's waterways. This invasive plant can grow up to 20cm a day during summer, forming dense patches that clog up the navigation. It also disrupts aquatic ecosystems by draining oxygen and out-competing native species. A smart biocontrol method has been to release its natural enemy, South American weevil, to manage the pest. To help reduce the spread of the plant, always check, clean and dry your equipment after paddling and volunteer for local removal initiatives. Every effort counts.

NEED TO KNOW

■ The Environment Agency (EA) manages the non-tidal section of the River Thames. Paddle craft must be registered with the EA or you can use Paddle UK's 'On The Water' membership.

■ The National Trust is the navigation authority for the River Wey Navigation. Their website has a guide for users of portable craft. A licence is required, but Paddle UK's 'On The Water' membership covers this waterway as well.

■ The Thames Lock is manned and there is a helpful National Trust information point. You may be asked for your waterways licence.

■ Check the conditions for the Thames (gov.uk/guidance/river-thames-current-river-conditions) and the Wey Navigation (riverweyconditionsnt.wordpress.com). Ensure the River Wey flow rate and water levels are suitable for paddling on the GOV.UK site or a river app.

Tuck in
- **Weybridge:** Little Gem Coffee at the Elmbridge Canoe Club and D'Oyly's Cafe on the island opposite. Short walk away, Old Crown and The Minnow. Many places to eat and drink in Weybridge town centre.
- **Along the way:** The Ferry Coffee Shop at Shepperton Lock.

Paddle providers

Elmbridge Canoe Club – elmbridgecanoeclub.com
Paddle Up – paddleup.co.uk

06 HAMPTON TO MOLESEY AND THAMES AITS

This route takes you to the original AquaPaddle location, Hampton – Molesey, on the non-tidal Thames. AquaPaddle is a free, timed 5km social paddle – think Parkrun but on the water. Join the event or paddle the course on your own, this stretch of the river is a classic Thames experience. Paddle around four historic islands where life moves at nature's pace, home to houseboats, bungalows, a sailing club, creative industries and even old boatyards. Welcome to Thames Riviera, complete with a touch of Shakespeare.

The Lowdown

DIFFICULTY

WATER TYPE River

LAUNCH/EXIT Riverbank

DISTANCE 5km (loop)

PORTAGES 0

LICENCE REQUIRED? Yes

START/FINISH
- ///bath.saves.curving (1) Hampton Bell Quay
- ///lives.anyone.shuts (2) Hurst Park
- Hampton (1) (National Rail) – 10-min walk
- Hurst Park Car Park (2), Molesey, West Molesey, KT8 1ST, height restriction 2.10m – free

A brief history

There are almost 200 islands on the Thames, known as 'aits' or 'eyots', both pronounced 'ate'. The terms seem to be specific to the Thames and simply mean small islands in a river. Many of the Thames islands formed naturally, while others emerged when locks, weirs and other navigation improvements were made. Their isolation and picturesque settings have historically attracted a variety of industries and activities, including boatbuilding, willow cultivation and country retreats for Londoners looking to escape the city.

The islands have colourful pasts, filled with intrigue and dramatic turns of events. There were lavish parties on Garrick's Ait, once part of actor David Garrick's 18th-century estate. Platt's Eyot gained fame for building naval ships, including the first aircraft carrier. And Tagg's Island was known for its grand hotel and glamorous guests. In more recent times, creative communities have blossomed on the islands, drawing artists, musicians and makers who appreciate the inspiring natural surroundings.

RIVER THAMES 47

RIGHT Garrick's Temple, a tribute to Shakespeare.

Today, many aits are inhabited, ranging from simple dwellings to luxury houseboats and bungalows, proof that you can live the island dream in London.

The paddle
Arriving by car, start at Hurst Park in the Surrey village of West Molesey, at the bottom of Sadlers Ride. Double win: free parking and a public toilet. Get onto the water from a concrete quay and paddle towards the Astoria houseboat on the Hampton side. Work your way upstream to your left to kick off the journey.

Paddle between the landscaped riverside and Garrick's Ait, formerly actor David Garrick's country retreat. Back in the 18th century he needed an entire island for entertaining – today it is private, with 20 bungalows only accessible by boat.

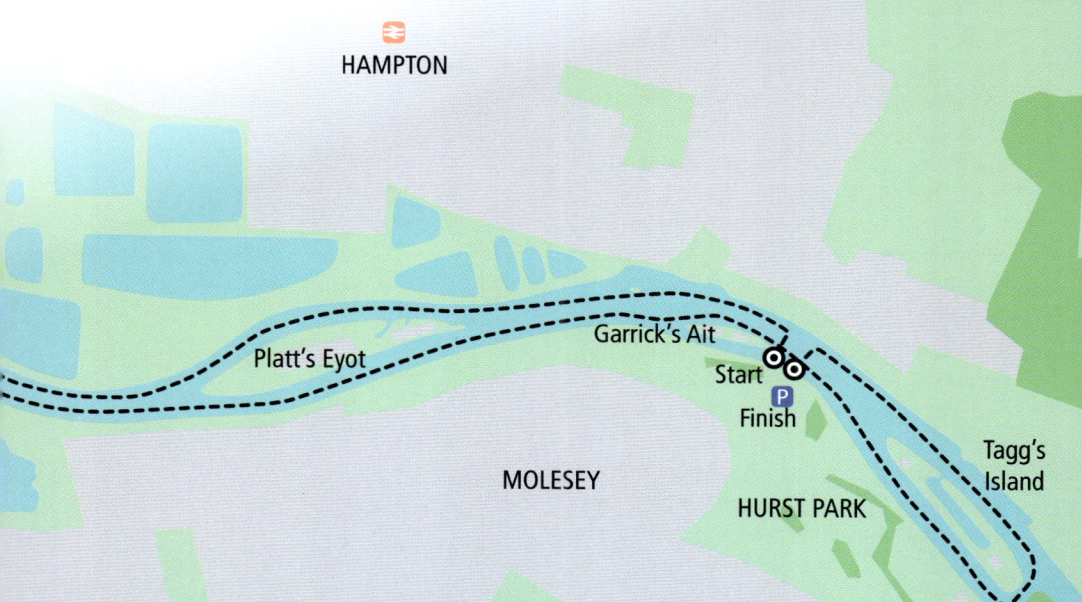

LEFT The Astoria houseboat, moored on the Thames in Hampton.

RIGHT An authentic Swiss chalet.

BELOW The original AquaPaddle location on the Thames.

Garrick's Lawn on the mainland welcomes the public, with its gardens restored to their former glory. The octagonal Garrick's Temple may be the world's only shrine to Shakespeare.

The slipway in front of Hampton Canoe Club is an alternative launch spot for this route, especially for those arriving by public transport. Hampton station is less than a 10-minute walk away. This also marks the official start and finish for AquaPaddle events. Soak up the classic riverside view of the Bell Inn pub and St Mary's Church, but mind the equally typical hustle and bustle on the water on summer weekends. The Hampton Ferry shuttles across the river and hires out boats. The tiny Benn's Island is home to the Hampton Sailing Club and there are also a few rowing clubs along the reach. It is all happening here.

Continue upstream towards the back channel at the tip of Platt's Eyot. Behind the trees lining the river, Hampton Water Treatment Works occupy a large site with filter beds, reservoirs and angular pumphouses. Thames Water operates the waterworks, which still supply about a third of London's water.

Up ahead, the green suspension footbridge links the private Platt's Eyot to the mainland. Unlike the smaller residential aits, Platt's is a

mix of contrasts: boatyards and industry on one end, wooded nature refuge on the other. There are even creative studios tucked away here. The entire island is lined by boats. As you paddle under the bridge, you can see the island's higher elevation – raised with gravel from the waterworks.

The upstream turnaround point for AquaPaddle is by the second ramp of Aquarius Sailing Club before the 2km mark. Cross the river and glide downstream. On the Surrey side, you may spot cattle grazing in the Molesey Reservoirs nature reserve, which used to be one of London's major water supplies. The Thames Path

hugs the river here, with a brief residential stretch before you return to the greenery of Hurst Park. Wave hello to Hampton Court Paddle Sports, a popular spot for local paddlers.

Leave the small passage for wildlife. Instead, follow the main channel past Garrick's Ait and then loop around Tagg's Island, the next private island downstream. After the small tree-covered islet, head right into the narrow stretch between East Molesey and Tagg's Island. There are no buildings here, but with 62 houseboats – most of them two-storey – it is without a doubt the best houseboat spotting on the Thames. Thames Riviera, some call it.

As you paddle around Tagg's, stay close to the island to avoid Ash Island's upstream weir in the main channel. At the downstream tip, take a sharp left before Ash Island, giving the weir on your right a wide berth for a safe return on the home stretch.

And yes, that is an authentic Swiss Chalet on the Hampton bank. Shipped from Switzerland in the 19th century, it was originally a boathouse but then converted into a modest five-floor family home. Paddle along St Albans Riverside under the road bridge connecting Tagg's

ABOVE Bridge connecting Tagg's to the mainland.

RIGHT Golden reflections at the end of the day.

Island to Hampton. Look left to see the entrance to a lagoon at the centre of the island. Unfortunately, access is limited to islanders only.

If you are chasing a personal best on the AquaPaddle route, it is time to sprint the final kilometre back upstream to Hampton Canoe Club.

Linking route

- 04 Windsor to Hampton Court

Wildlife highlight

Osier willow (*Salix viminalis*)
Willows are common on many Thames islands. Aits offered fine conditions for growing osier willows, with nutrient-rich flooding and no grazing cattle to contend with. Historically, they were cultivated to protect the islands from erosion and to supply materials for basket- and trap-making. Introduced to Britain in ancient times, this hardy non-native species is still

doing a good job in its adopted ecosystem. It provides shelter to wildlife and absorbs heavy metals. These days, the pliable reeds of osier are used in weaving sculptures.

Tuck in

- **At launch points:** Mobile coffee trailer at Hurst Park, The Bell Inn and Hampton Ferry Boathouse at Hampton Bell Quay.
- **Along the way:** Miss Polly Riverside café and Eight on the River café at Molesey Boat Club.

Paddle providers

AquaPaddle – aquapaddle.org
Dittons Paddle Boarding – dpbclub.co
Hampton Canoe Club – hamptoncanoeclub.org
Hampton Court Paddle Sports – hamptoncourtpaddlesports.com

NEED TO KNOW

■ The Environment Agency (EA) manages the non-tidal section of the River Thames. Paddle craft must be registered with the EA or you can use Paddle UK's 'On The Water' membership.

■ Always check the river conditions for the Thames before launching (gov.uk/guidance/river-thames-current-river-conditions).

■ Look up AquaPaddle dates for this location on their website.

■ If you are paddling on a Tuesday morning around 9, don't panic if you hear a siren – not the apocalypse, just the Hampton Waterworks testing their warning system.

07 THAMES DITTON TO RIVER EMBER

This paddle offers the leafy charm of a Surrey village, a Tudor backdrop and some backwater exploration right on the edge of Greater London. Launch from a riverside pub in Thames Ditton for a 6km route that takes you past Hampton Court Palace on the Thames, detours onto the River Ember, leads through a sluice tunnel and nips into a secret offtake. Is it a ditch? Maybe. Ideal for those who love discovering hidden waterways and do not mind a bit of off-roading. A perfect mini adventure for a summer's evening.

The Lowdown

DIFFICULTY

WATER TYPE River

LAUNCH/EXIT Jetty/river landing

DISTANCE 6km (return)

PORTAGES 1 x 2 (Molember sluice tunnel with rollers)

LICENCE REQUIRED? Yes

START/FINISH
- ///gets.tricks.answer
- Hampton Court (National Rail) – 15-min walk
- The Albany, Queens Rd, Thames Ditton KT7 0QY

A brief history

This stretch of the Thames is rich in Tudor history, with Hampton Court Palace at its centre. It saw Anne Boleyn's rise and fall from lady-in-waiting to Henry VIII's second wife, before her execution in 1536. Today, it is among the UK's top tourist attractions and host to many events, such as the Hampton Court Palace Festival in June and RHS Hampton Court Palace Garden Festival in July.

The second river on this route is the 3km Ember, a distributary of the Mole. Both

RIVER THAMES

waterways were historically used for milling. The River Mole splits to navigate around the Island Barn reservoir, the Mole running north while the Ember takes the southern side. The rivers have been rerouted to merge and join the Thames just downstream of Hampton Court Bridge, with additional changes made for flood prevention.

The paddle The adventure kicks off beside the Albany country pub on the Thames Ditton riverside, also home to Dittons Paddle Boarding. The site is ideal for arriving by car or about a 15-minute wander from the train station. From Queens Road, walk down to the river via a small passage on the left side of the pub. If you use the car park or facilities at

ABOVE Paddling past the backdrop of Hampton Court Palace.

LEFT The Albany riverside pub.

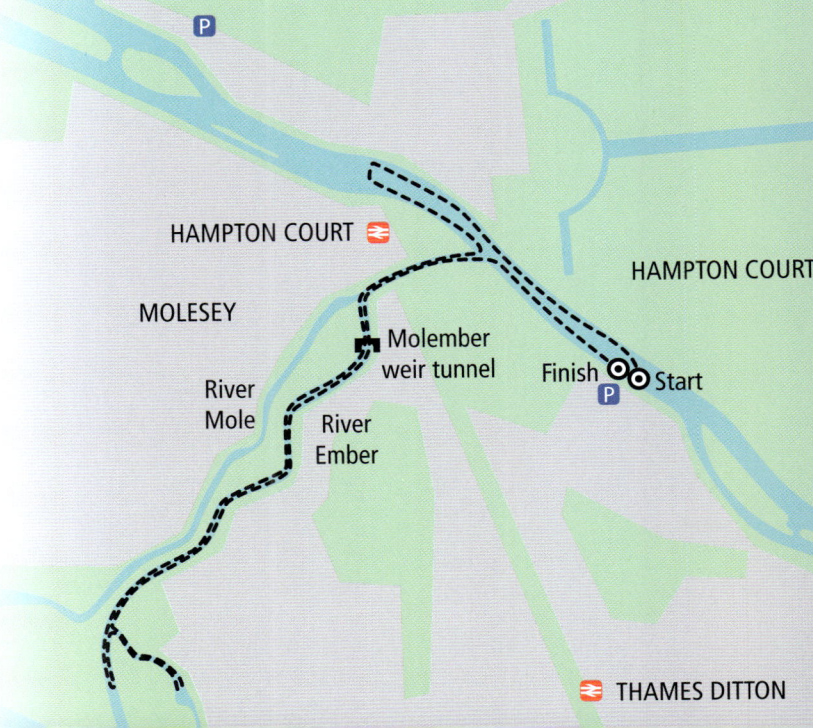

the Albany, it is only fair to grab a drink. Their gastropub menu may actually tempt you into something more after paddling.

Get onto the water from the jetty on the pub riverside and launch upstream, heading left towards Hampton Court Palace, just a kilometre away. The river flows between open grassland on both sides. The beach at Albany Reach Park gently slopes into the water. On sunny days, it is a popular spot for swimming, sunbathing and just about every water activity imaginable, even foiling. Anglers are always there, rain or shine.

Paddle in the direction of Hampton Court Bridge. You get a unique vantage point over one of London's six royal palaces, remarkably similar to what Henry VIII and his court would have seen when arriving by royal barge. Almost as if you slipped back to Tudor times. The Barge Walk separates the palace grounds from the river. Behind the decorative iron gates is Privy Garden. The Banqueting House is on the riverside with the backdrop of Hampton Court Palace, complete with red-brick towers and chimneys. All 241 of them, each a unique design.

Look out for river cruisers near the palace landing stage. Once you reach Hampton Court Bridge, turn around and cross the river to the opposite side. Paddle along Cigarette Island Park until the confluence of the Ember and Mole meet the river on your right. This is your cue to branch off the Thames to explore the lesser-known Ember.

The mood is immediately more urban – graffiti, a train platform and the distant hum of traffic. Pass under the railway and the A309 road bridges. The waterway splits into two here, the Mole boomed off and the Ember curving to the left. Stick to the River Ember to arrive in a basin where Molember Weir ends the journey for powered craft. For paddlers, no worries, in normal conditions you can portage through the sluice tunnel

on the left. Check any navigation signs before proceeding. Dismount carefully as the ramp is slippery and the tunnel is dark, with water flowing through it. Use the boat rollers if you are in a kayak or canoe. Pass through the tunnel before relaunching on the other side.

OPPOSITE TOP
Exploring the offtake of the Ember.

OPPOSITE BOTTOM
Molember sluice tunnel.

TOP RIGHT Boat rollers at Molember.

RIGHT Footbridge along the backwaters.

The Ember here has been engineered for flood prevention. On your left, the houses along Summer Road in Thames Ditton back onto this curious concrete channel, plenty of urban quirks to catch the eye. Across the way is Molember Road in East Molesey, River Mole running parallel but out of sight.

Follow the navigation under the Summer Road and Esher Road bridges and the surroundings start to feel more rural. About half a kilometre from Esher Road bridge, there is a concrete tunnel-like gap on the left, often frequented by anglers. This is the Ember's offtake. Ready for some off-roading?

The channel is overgrown and shallow, with reeds thriving in the muddy banks and branches dipping low. Paddling along the original course of the Ember is like stumbling into a hidden world. The water is surprisingly clear and you can see fish darting below. You may have to hop off and walk the shallow bits, passing a red-brick building on your left and slipping under Orchard Lane footbridge until you reach Imber Court Cottage on your right. You arrive at a dead-end pool. Now just two little streams, the waterway used to split here and the site in between housed Ember Mills until the mid-19th century. It is like a Zen retreat, just waiting for the soothing sounds of a gong. But now it is time to turn back.

At the main Ember channel, take a left and paddle until you see the next weir from a safe distance. This is your turnaround point. From here, it is a 2km journey to return to the pub. Once back on the main river, turn right and head to the Albany for a well-deserved post-paddle snack.

Linking route

- 08 Kingston to Hampton Court

Wildlife highlight

American mink (*Neovison vison*)
The American mink arrived in the UK in the 1920s for the fur trade. Fur farming in England was finally banned in 2000, but mink had already made themselves at home in the wild. Without any natural predators, they spread rapidly. These semi-aquatic

RIVER THAMES

creatures like scrubby riversides and canal banks for their dens and will hunt just about anything they can catch – fish, birds and small mammals, you name it. One of mink's favourite targets is the native water vole, which has been driven close to extinction. To protect water vole populations, humane mink control measures have been introduced, including the use of floating mink rafts here along the River Ember.

Tuck in
- The Albany pub at the launch point.
- Along the way, The Mitre hotel by Hampton Court Bridge.

Paddle providers
- Dittons Paddle Boarding – dpbclub.co
- Hampton Court Paddle Sports – hamptoncourtpaddlesports.com
- Paddle Up – paddleup.co.uk
- The SUP Adventure Girl – thesupadventuregirl.co.uk

OPPOSITE Turning onto the Ember and Mole.

ABOVE Backwater tranquillity.

NEED TO KNOW

■ The Environment Agency (EA) manages the non-tidal section of the River Thames. Paddle craft must be registered with the EA or you can use Paddle UK's 'On The Water' membership.

■ Always check the river conditions for the Thames before launching (gov.uk/guidance/river-thames-current-river-conditions).

■ For the River Mole, no licence is required. The engineered channel of the Ember is private, but Paddle UK members have an agreement that allows them to use this stretch. The Molember sluice tunnel is operated by the EA.

08 KINGSTON TO HAMPTON COURT

This cracking 10km route on the non-tidal Thames from Kingston to Hampton Court Palace delivers history and nature in equal measure. Often better known for retail therapy, launch from Kingston, paddling past houseboats, historic bridges and Thames aits. Just be prepared for some river traffic. Arrive at Hampton Court Palace in true Henry VIII style, then paddle back through peaceful backwaters for a close-up look at island life. With Tudor views, hidden tributaries, riverside pubs and punts along the way, this paddle offers both adventure and relaxation.

The Lowdown

DIFFICULTY

WATER TYPE River

LAUNCH/EXIT Riverbank

DISTANCE 10km (return)

PORTAGES 0

LICENCE REQUIRED? Yes

START/FINISH
///pencil.hiding.oasis
Kingston (National Rail) – 10-min walk
Thameside Car Park, Thames Side, Kingston upon Thames KT1 1PL – 5-min walk

BELOW Kingston Bridge, a landmark on the Thames.

RIVER THAMES

A brief history

The River Thames and royalty are central to Kingston's story, shaping its history and character. The route to Hampton Court Palace has been travelled for centuries. The river was like a regal motorway, kings and queens travelling between their residences. Henry VIII even had the Kingston Reach widened and straightened – perhaps to make his commute more spectacular. The Thames turned Kingston into a busy market town, connecting it to London and the world beyond.

There is something for SUP history buffs, too. Since 2007, thanks to Brian Johncey, paddleboards have been a familiar sight on these waters. He founded the Blue Chip SUPer Club, exploring waters local and afar. Brian went on to launch London's first SUP race, Battle of the Thames, opening the sport to a wider audience. Surbiton is even home to SUP Polo, featuring a world series tournament.

ABOVE Action-packed SUP polo.

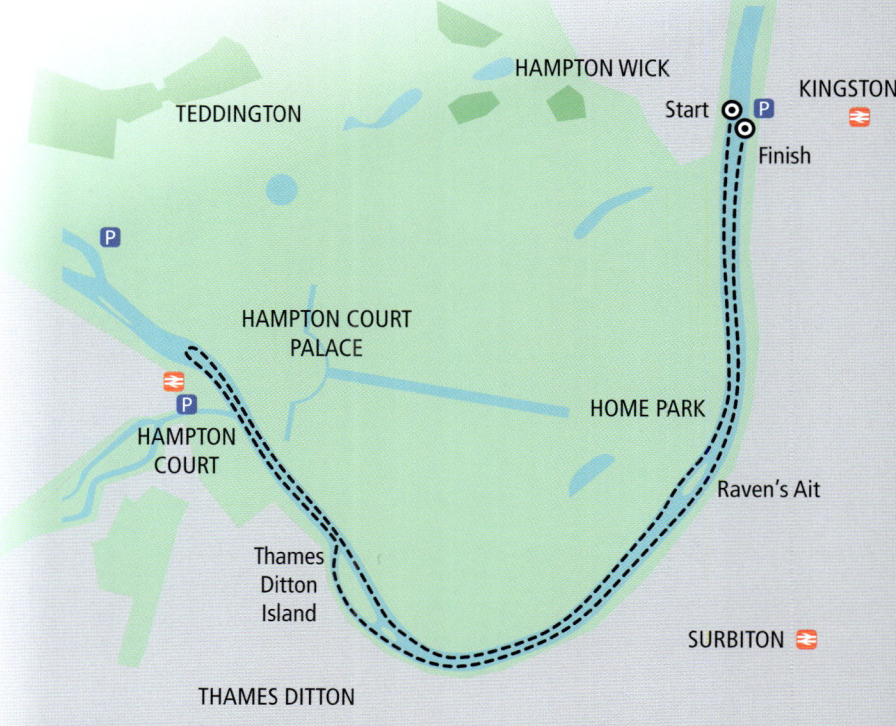

The paddle

Kingston attracts big crowds for shopping and entertainment. If you are driving, be prepared for the one-way traffic system. It can have you going in circles. Aim for the Thameside Car Park, but there are also plenty of options near the Bentall Centre. If you prefer to avoid the car chaos altogether, the walk from Kingston station is easy. Head towards Kingston Railway Bridge, where the launch spot is just downstream at Canbury Gardens. The river here is wide, but on sunny days it is like Costa del Kingston, always wake to contend with. Cross carefully to the Hampton Wick side before paddling upstream to Hampton Court Palace.

Past Kingston Bridge, the route runs beside the historic Barge Walk, part of the Hampton Court estate for over five hundred years. The path follows the river all the way to the palace, Home Park the scenic backdrop on the right the entire 5km stretch. The riverside is a mix of meadows and trees, lined with houseboats. People often lounge along the river here, picnicking and soaking in the views of the Thames and town centre across the water. Kingston's picturesque market square is just out of view.

Keep paddling. The first island on this route is Raven's Ait before the 2km mark in Surbiton. The island used to be called Raven's Arse, which would not be entirely fitting for its current function as an events venue. Opposite is Thames Sailing Club, home to the Blue Chip SUPer Club and their SUP polo pitch. Fancy a break? Harts Boatyard is next door for a drink and facilities.

Paddle upstream past the concrete-edged section with some random boat moorings. This site along Portsmouth Road used to be part of a Victorian waterworks. The old filter beds supplied London with clean water, but today it is a nature reserve. The Thames meanders in a gentle U-shaped bend alongside a golf course and parkland, once royal hunting grounds. And yes, fallow deer still roam freely here. Stick to the right, as you share the river with hire boats, pleasure cruisers and tour boats.

At the southern tip of the bend is Thames Ditton Marina, where boat moorings line the river. Their Hideaway restaurant is worth checking out. Another little river flows into the Thames behind the pontoons here. The Rythe runs through woodlands further up but is culverted through the more residential section around the Dittons.

BELOW Kingston is a mix of history and modern life.

As you approach the final 1.5km stretch before the turning point, paddle past a trio of linear islands. These were created when Henry VIII had the river widened for his commute to the palace. Today, all three are privately owned: Boyle Farm Island with its single cottage, tiny Swan Island in the middle and Thames Ditton Island like a village with nearly fifty houses, the river an extension of their gardens.

The classic pastime of punting is alive and well at Dittons Skiff and Punting Club, with tasters available weekly. After passing the Albany pub, the red-brick façade of Hampton Court Palace comes into view. It feels surreal to be paddling past Henry VIII's favourite palace, with its elaborate gates, many chimneys and formal gardens. Like a Tudor time capsule. To take a closer look on dry land, get off the water downstream of the landing stage or right by Hampton Court Bridge. Alternatively, cross the river and find a spot at Cigarette Island Park, next to where the Mole and Ember (see route 07) meet the Thames. Enjoy the royal views of Hampton Court Palace before heading back to Kingston.

ABOVE Thames Ditton footbridge.
BELOW Arriving at Hampton Court Palace.

On the return trip, explore the Thames Ditton Island backwaters. Shortly after the Albany, a narrow channel branches off to the right – navigate carefully, as it is one-way upstream for powered craft. GoBoat operates here, so you may spot a few first-

ABOVE Great food at the Mezzet Box.

time boaters. This hidden stretch gives you a close-up of island life, with homes ranging from quaint cottages on stilts to minimalist modern designs. Which villa would you choose? The car-free island is linked to Thames Ditton village by a footbridge, with the historic Ye Olde Swan at the base, another possible riverside pub stop.

Join the main channel again. Follow the river downstream, enjoying the gentle flow back towards Kingston to complete your royal route.

Linking routes
- 07 Thames Ditton to River Ember
- 09 Kingston to Teddington

Wildlife highlight

Ring-necked parakeet (*Psittacula krameri*) Native to India and Africa, the ring-necked parakeets are so common along this section of the Thames that they are called Kingston parakeets. Their vocal presence makes them easy to notice before you spot the exotic bright-green birds. There are plenty of theories about how parakeets made London their home, from 'The African Queen' film set to Jimi Hendrix releasing some, even a burglary at George Michael's house. The reality is probably less exciting – multiple escapes and releases, likely boosted by parrot fever. Look for them in treetops, especially in late summer and autumn, feasting on seeds, fruit and flowers. Whether parakeets are harming the local ecosystem is still up for debate.

Tuck in
Kingston town centre and the riverside upstream have plenty of spots to refuel. Along your route, you will pass Ginger Bees Café, Harts Boatyard, Hideaway, Ye Olde Swan and The Albany. Near Hampton Court, check out The Mitre and Mezzet Box, both on the water, plus several other places to eat and drink in Molesey, especially on Bridge Road.

Paddle providers
- **Dittons Paddle Boarding** – dpbclub.co
- **The Real Blue Chip SUPer Club** – bluechipsuperclub.co.uk
- **SUPolo** – worldseriessupolo.com

NEED TO KNOW

■ The Environment Agency (EA) manages the non-tidal section of the River Thames. For navigational information, consult 'The Thames Cruising Guide'. Paddle craft must be registered with the EA or you can use Paddle UK's 'On The Water' membership.

■ Before launching, check river conditions (gov.uk/guidance/river-thames-current-river-conditions).

■ Be aware that navigation may be restricted or closed due to repairs or events. For updates, visit www.gov.uk/guidance/river-thames-restrictions-and-closures.

RIVER THAMES 63

09 KINGSTON TO TEDDINGTON

This 5.5km round trip packs in urban charm with classic riverside scenery. Launch from Kingston upon Thames, London's oldest royal borough, and paddle downstream to Teddington Lock. Slip into the tranquil backwaters of Trowlock Island before a final loop into Kingston town centre, where the Hogsmill River meets the Thames. Along the way, expect rowers slicing through the water, hire boats cruising by and a committee of curious swans.

The Lowdown

DIFFICULTY 💧💧
WATER TYPE River
LAUNCH/EXIT Riverbank
DISTANCE 5.5km (return)
PORTAGES 0

LICENCE REQUIRED? Yes
START/FINISH
📍 ///funds.trucks.juices
🚉 Kingston (National Rail) – 10-min walk
🅿️ Thameside Car Park, Thames Side, Kingston upon Thames KT1 1PL – 10-min walk

A brief history

The name says it all – Kingston upon Thames. Dating back to Saxon times, Kingston was called 'Cyninges tun', meaning the king's manor in Old English. Seven Anglo-Saxon kings are said to have been crowned here, with the Coronation Stone still standing outside the Guildhall. Kingston's royal significance even earned it the title of England's first official royal borough.

Kingston's location on the River Thames was no coincidence either. The river linked the town to London and beyond, helping it develop into a commercial hub with a

ABOVE Paddling under Kingston Bridge.

ABOVE Paddling through Kingston.

The paddle

'Out of Order' is the name of the sculpture of 12 tumbling telephone boxes on Old London Road. It is a Kingston landmark not to be missed if you are walking to the river from the train station. Make your way to the Boaters Inn on the Thames riverside and find a good launch spot on the Canbury Gardens banks.

Set off downstream, away from the town centre. Use the main channel at Steven's Eyot, following the navigation markers. In Victorian times, this little island was a popular picnic spot and at one point a public swimming area for men, in the nude no less. It is private now, used by the Small Boat Club. As you paddle further, there is plenty of activity at sailing, rowing and canoe clubs on both sides. Not just the usual suspects – you may also catch the wash of dragon boats or outrigger canoes. Tempted?

Pass Trowlock Island to your left. The river widens and the greenery deepens, creating a rural feel. The Thames Path tails the water on the right. Teddington Lock and Weir is up ahead. The navigation leads to three locks and a portage point to continue downstream to the tidal section of the Thames. This route, however, takes you back to Kingston. Turn around well before the weir and cross over to navigate on the right. Look out for the resident cormorant, often sitting at the top of one of the poles. The banks belong to The Lensbury, an upmarket sports club and resort, built by Shell for its employees.

At the downstream end of Trowlock Island, take a quiet detour into the backwater. It is safe to ignore the 'No Navigation' signs, they do not apply to paddled craft. This passage

busy market and river trade. Before 1729, Kingston Bridge was the only crossing between London and Staines. The smaller Hogsmill River also played its part by powering five local mills and supporting industries in the area.

More recently, Teddington has been the finish line of the Thames 200 Ultra, a 200km ultra-paddle race down the navigable Thames from Lechlade, open to all paddle craft.

RIVER THAMES

is calm and peaceful, with overhanging vegetation and secluded bungalows, gardens sweeping to the water's edge. Glide through this hidden retreat and pass the hand-operated chain ferry at the end of the island before rejoining the main river. The Royal Canoe Club is the oldest in the world.

Urban paddling is about contrasts. As you paddle back, Kingston's urban side begins to emerge. Before the railway bridge, the grandeur of old riverside homes in Hampton Wick on your right meet the more modern skyline of Kingston on the left. Paddle under Kingston Railway Bridge, then continue under the five-arched Kingston Bridge. Once the first Thames crossing upstream after London Bridge, it is a good photo opportunity. The quayside here is a mix of houseboats, industry and new developments.

ABOVE The magic of backwaters at Trowlock Island.

BELOW Past the footbridge and Teddington Lock, the river turns tidal.

ABOVE Hogsmill River meets the Thames in Kingston.

Welcome to Costa del Kingston. On sunny weekends, waterfront open-air cafés and restaurants are buzzing with people. You cannot escape the crowds on the water either. Navigate carefully with vintage paddle steamers, rental boats, narrowboats and pleasure cruisers on the river – not all expertly handled. Keep clear of the traffic and make your way towards the mouth of the Hogsmill River, about 250m after Kingston Bridge.

Carefully cross the Thames, avoiding swans, and enter the Hogsmill, a quieter tributary. Paddle under three small bridges until you reach the historic Clattern Bridge, built around 1175 and one of the oldest road bridges in England. Turn around here and glide back to the main channel.

The final stretch leads you back to Canbury Gardens, wrapping up a route that combines history, nature and urban life – the essence of paddling in Kingston.

Linking routes

- 08 Kingston to Hampton Court
- 10 Ham House to Teddington Lock

Wildlife highlight

Water vole (*Arvicola amphibius*)
Remember Ratty from 'The Wind in the Willows'? He was actually a water vole. Once common across the UK, these endearing creatures have nearly vanished, with populations declining by more than 90 per cent since the 1950s. Why? Mainly because of predation by the invasive American mink. Mink are not necessarily strong swimmers, but can follow water voles into their burrows, leaving no escape. But there's hope. Along the Hogsmill River in Kingston, water voles are making a comeback as a result of Citizen Zoo's rewilding project. Keep your eyes peeled and listen for that signature 'plop' as they dive into the river, especially between April and September.

Tuck in

The Boaters Inn and Canbury Secret Café at Canbury Gardens. Many places to eat and drink in Kingston town centre and upstream of the launch spot.

Paddle providers

- **Albany Outdoors** – albanyoutdoors.org.uk
- **Paddle Up** – paddleup.co.uk
- **Royal Canoe Club** – royalcanoeclub.co.uk
- **Lensbury Watersports Centre** – lensbury.com
- **Thames 200 Ultra** – thames200ultra.com

NEED TO KNOW

■ The Environment Agency (EA) manages the non-tidal section of the River Thames. Paddle craft must be registered with the EA or you can use Paddle UK's 'On The Water' membership.

■ Check the river conditions for the Thames (gov.uk/guidance/river-thames-current-river-conditions) before launching.

10 HAM HOUSE TO TEDDINGTON LOCK

This scenic 5km paddle between Richmond and Teddington offers a wide stretch of the Thames rich with history, boatyards, islands and green spaces. Starting in Ham with the rare bonus of free parking, paddle past Eel Pie Island to Teddington Lock, where the tidal and non-tidal Thames meet. Along the way, explore the riverside life of modern Twickenham, with rowers, houseboats and leisure craft enjoying the water. It is a no-portage round trip, ideal for a peaceful escape – though summer weekends tend to get busy.

The Lowdown

DIFFICULTY ●●

WATER TYPE Tidal river

LAUNCH Draw Dock

DISTANCE 5km (round trip)

PORTAGES 0

LICENCE REQUIRED? No

START/FINISH
- ///plant.stays.pose
- Richmond (District Line, Mildmay, National Rail) + bus 65/371 – 10-min walk
- Ham Street Car Park, Ham Street, Richmond TW10 7RS, height restriction 2.73m – free

A brief history

Holiday vibe and leisure have long characterised this stretch of the Thames. Ham House, a 17th-century mansion, used to be a country retreat for royalty and nobility. Just upstream in Twickenham, Eel Pie Island became a 19th-century holiday destination, attracting Londoners with its hotel and chalets. Mostly famed for its legendary gigs, the island was previously a prime escape for those seeking a break from city life.

Yet, this was also a working river. Teddington Lock, first built in 1811, regulated the tidal flow and stabilised

ABOVE Eel Pie Island charm.

water levels upstream. It made the river non-tidal above Teddington. By the late 19th century, Richmond Lock and Weir was constructed to keep the stretch up to Teddington navigable even at low tides. The area also has strong boatmaking traditions, with boatyards on Eel Pie Island, active since the late 1800s, still handcrafting and restoring boats today.

ABOVE The White Swan, a classic riverside pub.

The paddle

It is a stately start to a paddle trip. Drive down Ham Street, past the 17th-century Ham House and Garden, now a National Trust estate. Parking could not be easier. Ham Street car park is free of charge and right next to the river at the bottom of the street.

Your launch spot is a former ferry landing with good visibility both ways. The wide-open river gives a sense of adventure. Just downstream, Hammertons Ferry may be shuttling between Ham and Marble Hill House. Cross the river carefully and head upstream towards Teddington. Stick to the right-hand side, taking the sheltered back channel between Eel Pie Island and Twickenham Embankment.

Too early for a break? Keep The White Swan pub in mind for the return leg. Paddle past the walled York House Gardens and the tower of St Mary's Church, before reaching Twickenham riverside. Tucked away is the old main road, Church Street, a local favourite for shopping, drinks and dining. The river here is lined with rowing and yachting clubs, so it can get busy on the water. Pass the Eel Pie boatyards. Admire the working front of the island, old-world craftmanship still alive and well. Glide under the narrow footbridge that connects the island to the mainland.

Back in the main channel, Ham Lands' greenery on the left hides the Thames Path, which runs along the river to Teddington. On the opposite bank are lovely riverside homes, including Thames Eyot and Cross Deep.

Don't be surprised if you see a Ganesh floating by. The Thames has been considered a sacred river for London's Hindu community since the 1970s and there are boats offering ash scattering services in the area.

After passing Radnor Gardens and its graceful weeping willows, cruise past Swan Island. Once just a mudflat, it was built up with clay from the excavation of the London Underground. It is called London Clay. Today, it is home to a boatyard and a small houseboat community.

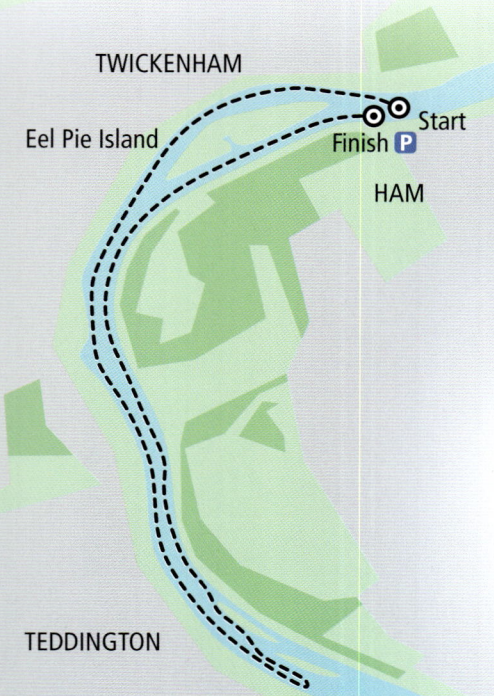

RIVER THAMES

ABOVE Summer days at Teddington.

See a small opening on the left? It opens up to a lagoon, connected to the river by a sluice. Historically a site for gravel workings, it is now part of Thames Young Mariners, an outdoor learning centre. On lower tide, a few shingle beaches appear on the foreshore. Teddington Bluetits swim here all year round.

Approaching the halfway point in Teddington, look for the obelisk on the opposite bank, marking the boundary between the Port of London Authority and the Environment Agency's jurisdiction upstream. You are arriving at the largest lock system on the Thames. It is a complex of three locks and a weir that controls the flow between the tidal and non-tidal river. Some say the name Teddington comes from 'Tide End Town'. Stay clear of pontoon moorings and give space for boats navigating in and out of the locks.

Lock Island on the left was cut from the Surrey bank. It features a red-brick cottage and manicured lawns. Pass the barge lock for larger boats, launch and skiff locks and finally, the portage point for paddlers. If you fancy a break, use the portage landing or exit the water at Ferry Road before the suspension footbridge. Or moor up at The Anglers' jetty, their garden rolling down to the river.

For the return, paddle back via the main channel by Eel Pie Island. Ham House also marks the finish line of the annual Great River Race, where hundreds of traditional boats row from London's Docklands, usually in late September. Once on dry land, pop by the Palm Centre or Petersham Nurseries for some garden inspiration, if plants are your thing.

ABOVE Paddling through riverside greenery.

Linking routes

- 09 Kingston to Teddington
- 11 Richmond to Eel Pie Island

Wildlife highlight

Red-eared terrapin
(*Trachemys scripta elegans*)
The restored quarry pits in Ham, now a Local Nature Reserve, are home to a variety of wildlife. The red-eared terrapins you may spot basking in the sun didn't arrive here by accident. They are the legacy of the 80s and 90s Teenage Mutant Ninja Turtles craze. Remember Leonardo, Donatello, Raphael and Michelangelo? These tiny terrapins were popular in pet trade, costing around £2, only to grow into dinner-plate-sized giants, often abandoned illegally in the wild. Surprisingly resilient, this non-native species has adapted to survive in the Thames and London's canals. While terrapins are not confirmed to be breeding, they can be seen from spring to autumn. Report sightings to the National Centre for Reptile Welfare.

ABOVE Riverside views at Teddington.

Tuck in

- The Orangery Café at Ham House (for National Trust members).
- Along the way, The White Swan, Barmy Arms on Twickenham riverside, plenty of options along Church Street and in Twickenham town centre.
- At Teddington riverside, The Albany, Flying Cloud Cafe and pubs on Ferry Road.

Paddle providers

- **The London Stand Up Paddle Co** – standuppaddle.london
- **Paddle Richmond** – paddlerichmond.co.uk
- **Back of Beyond Adventures** – backofbeyonduk.com

NEED TO KNOW

■ The Port of London Authority (PLA) manage the tidal Thames below Teddington Lock. Before setting out, read the Tideway Code on their website for important rules and etiquette. Always check the PLA ebb flag tide before getting on the water.

■ Understanding of tides and river flow is critical for safety on this stretch. Restrict outings to half-tide times when the Richmond Lock weir gates are closed, typically from about two hours after high water until two hours before the next high tide. Stay clear of moored boats, pontoons and any obstructions to avoid risk of pinning and entrapment. Check the river flow at Kingston. While the rate may be within a normal range, it can still be strong and challenging for paddling.

■ If you plan to paddle between October and November, check the annual draw-off dates for Richmond Lock, as the conditions might be better suited for mudlarking rather than paddling.

11 RICHMOND TO EEL PIE ISLAND

This scenic paddle on the tidal section of the River Thames covers views that have inspired many artists and writers. There are period estates and lush gardens, wide green spaces and charming riverside pubs. The route combines the tranquillity of countryside with the urban chic of south-west London. Richmond, named the happiest place to live in Britain, sets the stage with cobbled lanes and independent shops. The circular paddle takes you around Eel Pie Island in Twickenham and back to Richmond.

The Lowdown

- **DIFFICULTY** ●●
- **WATER TYPE** Tidal river
- **LAUNCH** Draw dock
- **DISTANCE** 5km (round trip)
- **PORTAGES** 0
- **LICENCE REQUIRED?** No
- **START/FINISH**
  - ///organ.sunset.void
  - Richmond (District Line, Mildmay, National Rail) – 10-min walk
  - Friars Lane Car Park, Friars Ln, Richmond TW9 1NL – 5-min walk

A brief history
Richmond's history has been shaped by kings and queens since Tudor times. Henry VII established Richmond Palace in the early 16th century. The riverside location made it easy for the royal family to travel to and from London.

Over time, Richmond became a popular spot for tourists seeking a getaway close to the capital. It has always been a magnet for the rich and famous. Great for celebrity spotting, Richmond's residents have included Sir David Attenborough, Sir Mick Jagger, Tom Hardy and, of course, the fictional Ted Lasso.

ABOVE Boat hire in Richmond.

Eel Pie Island off the banks of Twickenham emerged as a music hotspot in the 60s. The iconic Eel Pie Island Hotel was the place to be, drawing in legends like The Rolling Stones, Pink Floyd, Eric Clapton and The Who. The venue was destroyed in a fire, but the island still holds secrets of its legendary parties.

The paddle

Unless you opt for an early bird adventure, Richmond riverside is alive with people. There are crowds spilling out from waterfront pubs, restaurants and cafés – drinking, eating, lounging, strolling or watching the world slip idly by. At the end of the cobbled Water Lane is a draw dock, located between the White Cross and Slug & Lettuce. It's a great launch spot. While you are pumping up your board, expect casual chats with curious passers-by. Striking up conversations with complete strangers often adds to the charm of urban paddling.

The foreshore changes with the tide, it is never the same. Footwear is recommended because of unexpected surprises on the riverbed. At low tide, be ready to wade in knee-deep water. Glide gently onto the water. Take your time to find your balance before crossing the river upstream, looking out for boat traffic.

Richmond Bridge dates back to 1777 and is the oldest surviving bridge on the Upper Thames. Its five arches span the river. Structures like this obstruct the natural ebb and flow of the river, creating eddies, swirls and turbulent water. Use the first available arch closest to the right bank to pass under the bridge.

Towpath follows the river on both sides. Because the river meanders so much above Putney, what would usually be identified as

ABOVE Ready to launch from Richmond.

LEFT LSUPCO paddlers in front of Corporation Island.

north and south banks are called Middlesex for the north and Surrey for the south. During the summer months, the pastoral scene is complete with cows grazing on Petersham Meadows, upstream on the Surrey side. Paddling here is like stepping into a painting and experiencing the scenery of JMW Turner's 'The Thames from Richmond Hill' on the water. This classic Thames view is in fact protected by an Act of Parliament, the only such view in England. Worth a photo!

Leaving the small Glover's Island on your left, Marble Hill House appears on the right. You are now on a beautiful tree-lined stretch known as Horse Reach. Wave hello to Hammertons Ferry, a family-operated ferry for pedestrians and cyclists. On the Surrey side, the historic Ham House and Garden is a National Trust site (see route 10).

Up ahead is Eel Pie Island. Veer off from the main channel towards the backwaters. The charming White Swan pub is often too tempting to pass without a break on their flower-clad patio right on the river. There is also a beach next to it in case you brought your own refreshments.

Paddle past York House Gardens and catch a glimpse of the eccentric Naked Ladies statue. Arriving at Twickenham Embankment, a narrow footbridge connects Eel Pie Island to the mainland. The island is home to working boatyards, twenty-something artists' studios, 50 houses and 120 residents. It is rare to get an opportunity to set foot on this private island, but the bohemian quarter is open to the public twice a year, typically in July and December.

The wooded upstream tip of Eel Pie Island is a nature conservation area.

ABOVE The beautiful Richmond riverside.

Keeping a good lookout, cross back to the main channel and start the return journey along the Surrey side. The view of Richmond Hill and the Star and Garter building is amazing. This landmark, previously a hotel visited by famous figures like Dickens and Tennyson, is now an upmarket residential building.

is a firm favourite. In addition to brick-and-mortar venues, Richmond Duck Pond Market is an artisan market at Heron Square, which has street food stalls every weekend throughout the year.

Paddle providers

- **The London Stand Up Paddle Co** – standuppaddle.london
- **Paddle Richmond** – paddlerichmond.co.uk
- **Back of Beyond Adventures** – backofbeyonduk.com

LEFT The White Cross in Richmond with rock star parking.

Once back in Richmond riverside and on dry land, take a selfie with Virginia Woolf. Her full-size bronze statue sits on one of the benches on the Heron Square upper terraces, book in hand and smiling, overlooking the river.

Linking routes

- 10 Ham House to Teddington Lock
- 12 Kew Bridge to Richmond

Wildlife highlight

Grey heron (*Ardea cinerea*)
A lone heron frozen to immobility by the water's edge is a familiar sight on London paddles. But a whole colony? Opposite the launch point, the uninhabited Corporation Island is home to a long-established heronry. Their large stick nests sit high in the willow trees. Every February, they return to raise their young.

Tuck in

The riverside both in Richmond and Twickenham offers a wide variety of dining and refreshments options. The White Cross

NEED TO KNOW

■ The tidal Thames below Teddington Lock is controlled by the Port of London Authority (PLA). Make sure to read the Tideway Code on their website for essential rules and etiquette.

■ This route is not for beginners – you must understand tides and river flow. Restrict outings to half-tide times (typically two hours after high tide to two hours before), when Richmond Lock's weir gates are down. Always check the PLA ebb tide flag and do not paddle when flow rates are high or the river is in flood.

■ If planning an October–November adventure, note the annual draw-off. For about four weeks, the half-tide barrier at Richmond is left open for maintenance. This means that the river drains to its natural levels. It is as if someone has pulled the plug, leaving low water levels unsuitable for paddling.

12 KEW BRIDGE TO RICHMOND

London's country escape, this 5km one-way route offers scenic views of the Arcadian Thames between Kew Bridge and Richmond. It combines history, industry and urban life. Paddle past royal palaces, stately homes and parkland and explore the wilderness of back channels. Perfect for those familiar with tidal waters, comfortable with a bit of mud and prepared for a possible portage along the way.

The Lowdown

DIFFICULTY ●●●

WATER TYPE Tidal river

LAUNCH/EXIT Slipway/draw dock

DISTANCE 5km (one way)

PORTAGES 1 (Richmond Lock)

LICENCE REQUIRED? No

START
- ///lands.enjoyable.echo
- Kew Bridge (National Rail) – 3-min walk or Gunnersbury (District Line, Mildmay) – 15-min walk
- Limited on Strand on the Green, check parking apps for restrictions

FINISH
- ///organ.sunset.void
- Richmond (District Line, Mildmay, National Rail) – 10-min walk
- Friars Lane Car Park, Friars Ln, Richmond TW9 1NL – 5-min walk

A brief history

This corner of south-west London is rich in royal and aristocratic influence, with Richmond Palace, Kew Palace and Hampton Court Palace further upstream. Grand estates, gardens, parkland and hunting grounds flourished along the river during the 18th century, creating the Arcadian Thames, London's countryside. Industry left its mark too, with Brentford Gas Works and Kew Bridge Waterworks fuelling London's growth. By Victorian times, the once-exclusive riverside began drawing London's increasing

ABOVE Pebbly foreshore at Kew Bridge at low tide.

PADDLE LONDON

NEED TO KNOW

- The Port of London Authority (PLA) controls the tidal Thames below Teddington Lock. Check the Tideway Code on the PLA website.

- This route is for experienced paddlers only. Do not paddle alone. Understanding tides and river flow is crucial for safety. Paddle only when the river is not in flood or high flow. The best time to paddle this upstream route is at the start of the flood tide when you are assisted by the incoming tide.

- Always give way to boats, especially as the river gets very narrow at low water. They have limited ability to manoeuvre.

- This area is busy with rowers. Key rowing shouts to know: 'Take a look' and 'Look ahead'.

- Keep well clear of overhanging trees. Also watch for bridges, piers, buoys and moorings to avoid getting trapped and pinned, especially with strong tides.

- In the section between Putney and Syon Reach, paddle against the tide by 'working the slacks', using slower water on the inside of bends. Pre-arranged crossing zones let you switch to the left-hand side to stay in the slower flow. This applies only when paddling against the tide.

BELOW Winter mood on the water.

population seeking a retreat. Affordable railway tickets turned the rural riverside into a destination for all.

The paddle

A short walk from Kew Bridge station, the launch spot is on the north bank of the Thames, on the downstream side of Kew Bridge off the picturesque Strand on the Green. There is a public slipway onto the river. One of London's oldest SUP schools, Active360, has been operating from the bridge arches here since 2011. They offer everything from beginner lessons to club paddles and nature tours and know the river like the back of their hands.

In normal conditions, it is best to launch after low water as the incoming tide will help you along upstream. At low tide, more of the foreshore is exposed. The Thames mud sinks fast and claims flip-flops, so wear proper footwear. On a paddleboard, prepare to wade knee-deep into the river to launch.

The river can be busy with boats and rowers. On the opposite side is Kew Pier – trip boats gliding in at speed from downstream and turning around 360 degrees back onto the pier. Large vessels have limited manoeuvring ability, especially with the tidal stream, so keep your distance. Start your journey upstream through arch #1. Bridge arches are numbered starting from the north bank with arch #1. Navigate on the right.

The first island, or ait, on the route is Brentford Ait. If water levels allow, take the back channel on the right, then stick to the centre to avoid the shallows. To prevent grounding in the muddy riverbed, use your paddle to keep gauging the depth as you go. Return to the main channel if there is not enough water. The ait itself consists of two parts, with an unnavigable gap called Hog Hole in between. It is a bird sanctuary with willows, alders and poplars and owes its greenery to royal vanity. King George III had trees planted to shield Kew Palace from the

ABOVE Can you do a tree pose on a paddleboard?

industrial view of Brentford Gas Works.

Paddle under the blue footbridge that connects Lot's Ait to the Brentford bank. The island is home to a historic boatyard. Follow the backwater curving left and rejoin the main channel. Continue past the junction with the Grand Union Canal (see route 20) and you are on Syon Reach.

Next is another regal Thames stretch with Kew Palace, set within the Royal Botanic Gardens, on the left, and Syon Park on the right. If the tide has risen enough, you may see the Percy Lion that crowns Syon House. Along Syon's river frontage lies London's last natural tidal meadow, such a contrast to Kew Gardens' concrete embankment. The pink, domed Pavilion boathouse at Syon House was among the many river studies sketched by JMW Turner during his stay at the Ferry House.

On the Isleworth side, swans and Canada geese gather along the old ferry slipway and stone embankment. If you need a break, take your pick from the All Saints' church or the London Apprentice.

ABOVE Richmond Railway and Twickenham bridges.

Keep to the right and paddle another back channel at Isleworth Ait. It gives you a rare scene of the industrial waterfront with working boatyards off the ait. The wooded island is a Local Nature Reserve, and a no-landing zone. At the upstream tip, keep away from the residential marina at the River Crane junction.

The river opens up to reveal Richmond Lock and Weir, followed by Twickenham and railway bridges. The 19th-century weir structure spans between the Old Deer Park and St Margarets, with three sluice gates suspended from the footbridge. For about two hours around either side of high water, the gates are raised, letting boats and paddlers through freely. Just follow the arch signage. At other times, when the gates are down, boats pay £12 to use the lock, but human-powered craft can portage for free. The portage is under arch #1 on the far right. Stay clear of the weirs and be careful on the boat roller – it is always slippery.

After the bridges, Richmond's riverside unfolds in all its beauty: landscaped terraces, stately buildings, historic bridge and the famous Richmond Hill as the backdrop (see route 11). It is a busy stretch on the water, so give way to other craft and enjoy the scenery.

Around Flower Pot Islands, start to prepare your exit. Aim for the draw dock between the White Cross and Slug & Lettuce on the left, leaving Corporation Island on your right. Mind the trip boats coming and going from St Helena Pier. On sunny days, expect an audience. Safety first but finish in style.

Linking routes
- 11 Richmond to Eel Pie Island
- 13 Putney to Kew Bridge
- 14 Chelsea to Kew

Wildlife highlight
Tide Meadow at Syon Park
At first glance, this 1km river stretch at Syon Park in Brentford may not look like much. But the 21-hectare meadow, a designated Site of Special Scientific Interest (SSSI), is anything but ordinary. Flooded twice daily with the ebb and flow of the Thames, it is the last unbanked section of the river in Greater London. In a city where built development has tamed the river by straightening and narrowing the channel, added hard flood defences and disrupted intertidal habitats, the natural riverbank offers a refuge for wildlife. Among them is the German hairy snail (*Pseudotrichia rubiginosa*), found only in a handful of UK locations. The meadow is best seen from the river, a treat for paddlers on this route. Just do not expect to spot the snails.

ABOVE Backchannel at Isleworth Ait.

Tuck in
- At Kew Bridge, close to the launch spot, fuel up at One Over the Ait, Express Tavern, Strand Cafe, The Roastery or The Bell & Crown.
- Mid-route, take a break at the London Apprentice in Isleworth.
- At Richmond's finish line, the White Cross awaits, in addition to a spread of riverside and town centre spots. Spoilt for choice? Absolutely.

Paddle providers
- **Active360** – active360.co.uk
- **London Kayak School** – londonkayakschool.com
- **The London Stand Up Paddle Co** – standuppaddle.london
- **Paddle Richmond** – paddlerichmond.co.uk

BELOW High tide paddling at Richmond Lock.

13 PUTNEY TO KEW BRIDGE

This one-way route on the tidal Thames in south-west London covers the famous Cambridge-Oxford Boat Race course and more. It is a challenging section, suitable only for experienced paddlers due to busy navigation and strong tidal waters. From Putney, paddle upstream through the wider, meandering river through Hammersmith, Barnes, Mortlake and Chiswick, finishing in Kew. There are six picturesque bridges and two Thames aits here, along with countless riverside pubs. Enjoy the sense of spaciousness, like a country trip without leaving Zone 3.

The Lowdown

DIFFICULTY ●●●
WATER TYPE Tidal river
LAUNCH Slipway/draw dock
DISTANCE 8.5km (one way)
PORTAGES 0
LICENCE REQUIRED? No

START
- ///mouse.phones.flies
- Putney (National Rail) – 15-min walk, Putney Bridge (District Line) – 15-min walk or Putney Pier (River Bus) – 10-min walk
- Limited on Putney Embankment, check parking apps for restrictions

FINISH
- ///lands.enjoyable.echo
- Kew Bridge (National Rail) – 3-min walk or Gunnersbury (District Line, Mildmay) – 15-min walk
- Limited on Strand on the Green, check parking apps for restrictions

A brief history

Londoners have long escaped to leafy Putney for recreation. The horseshoe-shaped stretch of the Thames between Putney and Mortlake is one of the river's most famous sections. Since 1845, it has hosted the annual men's Boat Race between Oxford and

ABOVE Off we go.

ABOVE Putney Bridge.

Cambridge, with the women's race joining the same Championship Course in 2015. Held annually in March or April, the race runs upstream with the incoming tide. The start line at Putney Embankment is marked by a carved UBR (University Boat Race) stone and, more recently, a bronze strip set into the granite paving, inspired by the river itself.

This section of the Thames also features Fulham Palace and Hammersmith Bridge, one of the world's oldest suspension bridges.

The paddle

Choose a convenient launch spot on the rowing-club-lined Putney Embankment – the Leader's Gardens end is preferable. The Putney side of the river is known as Surrey, the Fulham side Middlesex. During weekends and in the summer, it is heaving with rowers carrying their boats – eights, sculls, fours, doubles and tin fish ready at the water's edge. The slipway is muddy and devious at low water. At a busy hub like this, take extra care when getting onto the water.

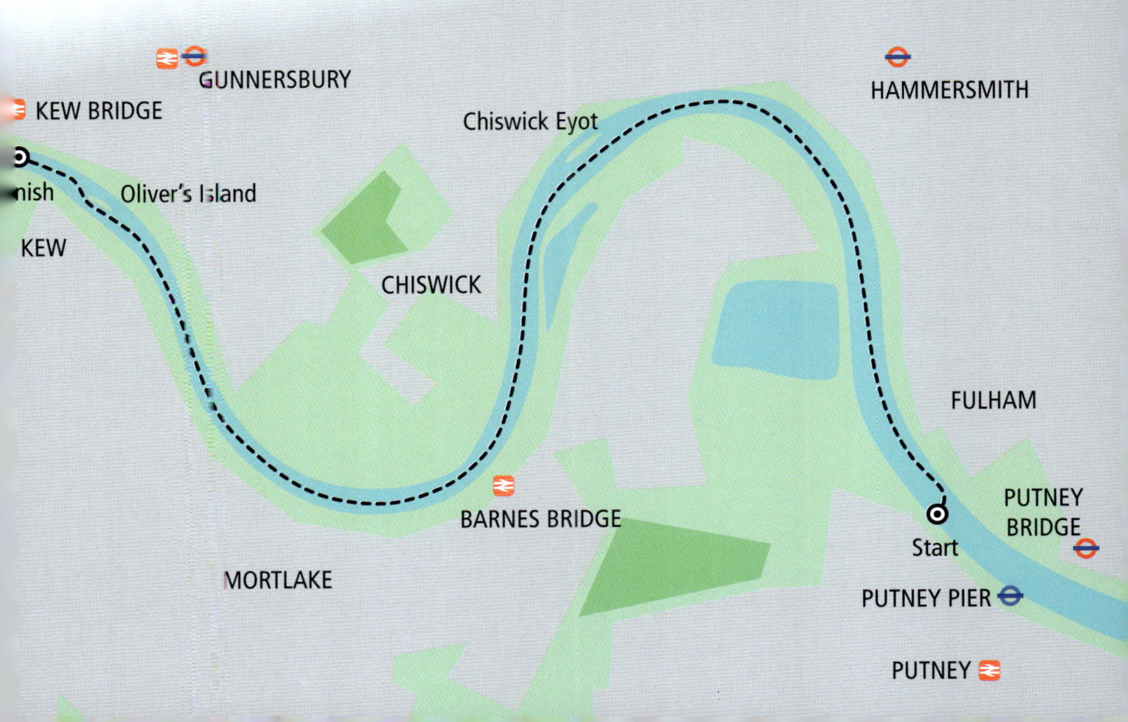

Leave Putney Bridge behind you, as paddleboarding is restricted below it. Stay close to the embankment past all the moorings, watching out for rowing crews. Cross to the Middlesex side when safe. Next to Bishops Park is the oldest football stadium in London, Craven Cottage. In front of it is a new riverside walkway, decking over the river, which opened in 2024.

Paddle under Hammersmith Bridge using the nearest available arch on the Middlesex bank. The Surrey side hides away the London Wetland Centre. It is like a secret wildlife oasis, formed of reclaimed Victorian reservoirs. Did you spot the Harrods Depository, now converted into luxury flats?

Continue towards Chiswick Reach. Make sure to avoid being pushed towards Dove Pier and the large barges as the river starts a steep curve left. The uninhabited Chiswick Eyot soon on your right is a nature reserve. At low tide, the ait is connected to Chiswick Mall but can strand visitors when the tide rises. The green pole is for boat race timing.

Before another river loop in the opposite direction, Chiswick Pier hosts an RNLI Lifeboat Station. The second busiest in the UK, they cover the river for search and rescue. Pass through Barnes, Mortlake and Chiswick, under Barnes Railway Bridge and Chiswick Bridge. Spot a bale of hay hanging from a bridge? It is an old rule signalling restricted headroom during works. Near The Ship pub, a stone marked UBR indicates the Boat Race finish line. Keep a good lookout in this hectic rowing and sailing area, and leave larger vessels to dominate the fairway. Correct positioning is essential.

On the final leg to Kew, Strand on the Green is picturesque, with quaint riverside houses and pubs. Past Kew Railway Bridge is another Thames ait, Oliver's Island. Stick to the Middlesex side and look out for speedy tour boats at Kew Pier. Get off the water at the public draw dock just downstream of Kew Bridge. That's the Boat Race course ticked off your list!

Linking routes

- 12 Kew Bridge to Richmond
- 14 Chelsea to Kew

Wildlife highlight

Grey seal (*Halichoerus grypus*)
Nearly four thousand seals call the Thames home. Grey seals are more common but the smaller harbour seals are also around. They are usually found in the estuary, where the river meets the North Sea. However, sightings upriver of Putney are on the rise. The brackish water here provides plenty of food for them.

If you meet a seal on the water, they might playfully pop up or even hop onto your craft. Admire these beautiful creatures at distance. Never touch or feed them – seals may bite if they feel threatened. If you spot a seal on the foreshore, give it space as they come ashore to rest, digest, moult or have their pups. Report the sighting to PLA Vessel Traffic Services, if you think the seal is in trouble.

OPPOSITE Fulham FC's new Riverside Stand at Craven Cottage.

RIGHT The joy of paddling.

Tuck in

The riverside between Putney and Kew is packed with pubs. If you take a pit stop, remember to secure your craft to avoid losing it to the tide.
Putney: Visit one of the several cafés on Lower Richmond Road or grab coffee and snacks on the Embankment. The Clubhouse is a favourite because every great adventure starts with good coffee.
Along the route: The Crabtree, The Blue Boat, The Blue Anchor, The Dove, Black Lion, Old Ship, The Watermans Arms, White Hart, The Ship, Bulls Head, The City Barge, The Bell & Crown, The Steam Packet.
Kew Bridge: One Over the Ait, The Express Tavern, Strand Cafe, The Roastery.

Paddle providers

- Active360 – active360.co.uk
- London Kayak School – londonkayakschool.com

NEED TO KNOW

■ The Port of London Authority (PLA) controls the tidal Thames below Teddington Lock. Check the Tideway Code for essential rules and etiquette on this challenging section.

■ This route is for experienced paddlers only. Do not paddle alone. Understanding tides and river flow is crucial for safety. Paddle only when the river is not in flood or high flow. The best time to paddle this upstream route is at the start of the flood tide when you are assisted by the incoming tide.

■ This area is busy with rowers and sailing boats. Rowers face backwards and may not see you, so avoid getting tangled with their oars. Key rowing shouts to know: 'Take a look' and 'Look ahead'.

■ Watch for bridges, piers, buoys and moorings to avoid getting trapped and pinned, especially with strong tides. Be aware that wind affects the river differently along its twisting course.

■ Paddle against the tide by 'working the slacks' and using the slower flow on the inside of bends. Designated crossing zones let you switch to the left-hand side. This applies to the entire route here, officially defined as Putney to Syon Reach in the Tideway Code.

14 CHELSEA TO KEW

Chelsea is an upmarket London neighbourhood with art, shopping and, of course, football. Its central location on the Thames makes it an iconic paddle location. An organised tour is the safest way to explore the fast-flowing Thames Tideway below Putney Bridge, where paddling is restricted by the Port of London Authority and risks are unique to Britain's busiest waterway. Suitable for experienced paddlers, the one-way route twists and turns from Chelsea through Battersea, Wandsworth, Fulham, Putney, Hammersmith and Barnes to Kew. There is a parade of architecture, historic sites, Thames Clippers, the odd helicopter and a series of bridges. **Top tip:** book on to a Guy Fawkes paddle with fireworks lighting up the river.

A brief history

Chelsea Waterworks Company was one of London's first water suppliers in the 18th century. Drinking water was drawn directly from the tidal Thames. By 1750, London was Europe's largest city, with a population of 750,000, and by 1850, that number had skyrocketed to over two million. With industrialisation and untreated human, household and industrial waste dumped into the river, waterborne diseases like cholera became inevitable.

To improve water quality, sand filtration was introduced and water intakes moved upstream to cleaner sections of the

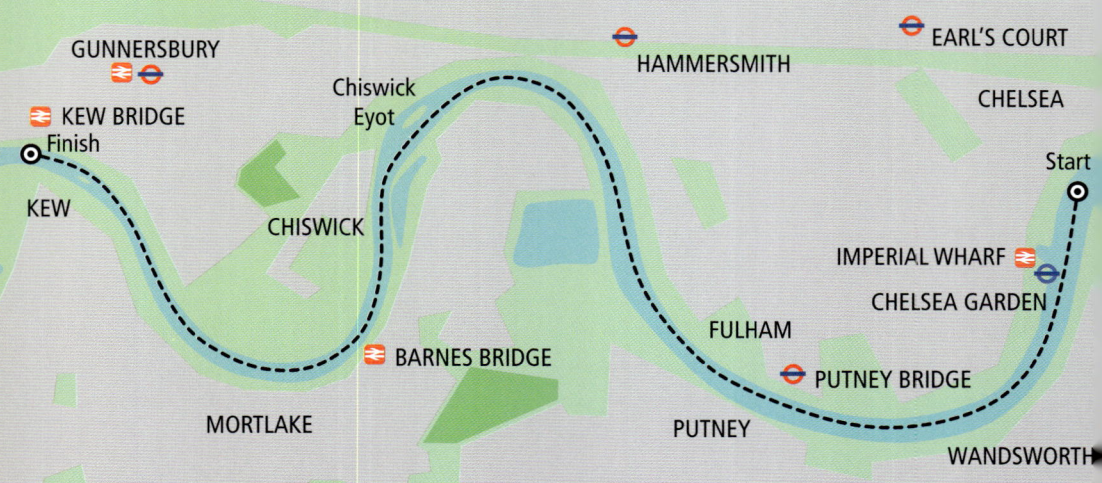

RIVER THAMES

ABOVE Preparing for the upstream journey.

Thames. The crisis peaked in 1858 with the Great Stink, leading to the creation of London's sewage system. Sir Joseph Bazalgette's comprehensive scheme is still in use today.

However, London's growth and climate change have pushed the Victorian system beyond its limits. During heavy rain, it overflows into the Thames. To tackle this, the Thames Tideway Tunnel, a 25km super sewer, was fully connected in 2025. With a capacity of 1.6 million cubic metres, equivalent to 600 Olympic-sized swimming pools, the tunnel is expected to prevent 95 per cent of spills by capturing excess storm sewage and transferring it to Beckton for treatment.

The Lowdown

DIFFICULTY 💧💧💧
WATER TYPE Tidal river
LAUNCH Foreshore/draw dock
DISTANCE 12.5km (one way)
PORTAGES 0
LICENCE REQUIRED? No, but restricted

START
- ///fumes.event.prone
- Earl's Court (District Line, Piccadilly Line) – 15-min walk; Imperial Wharf (Mildmay, National Rail) – 11-min walk; Chelsea Harbour Pier (River Bus) – 12-min walk
- Check parking apps

FINISH
- ///lands.enjoyable.echo
- Kew Bridge (National Rail) – 3-min walk; Gunnersbury (District Line, Mildmay) – 15-min walk
- Limited on Strand on the Green, check parking apps for restrictions

The paddle

The Tideway below Putney Bridge has restrictions for SUP, so this paddle can only be done as part of an instructor-led group unless specific requirements are met. Active360 runs guided paddles from London Sports Trust's site in Chelsea, giving you access to this section of the tidal Thames.

ABOVE Active360 SUP club out on the water.

Walking down Edith Grove takes you past a Banksy mural from the animal-themed series that emerged across London in August 2024. Cremorne Gardens, a popular pleasure ground in Victorian times, is located off Lots Road, just behind the King's Road. Enter through the ornate wrought-iron gates. An access ramp leads down to the riverside, where houseboats rest grounded at low tide in the Old Ferry Wharf. With a tidal range of up to 7m, the river has shrunk, revealing a pebbly foreshore and opening views of the skyline, marked by the glass towers and sleek apartments of Chelsea, Fulham and Battersea.

After a safety briefing, the group launches upstream, the water slack before the incoming tide comes to lend a hand. The guide reports the journey plan on VHF.

Over on the Battersea side, besides St Mary's Church (see route 15), it is all about riverside living. Paddle in the inshore zone, staying close to the right-hand side. The red-bricked Lots Road Power Station, which once powered the London Underground, is a Chelsea landmark. Like Bankside and Battersea power stations, it has been repurposed. Beside it, the muddy Chelsea Creek gives a clue about the area's industrial past, when Kensington Canal served the Imperial Gas Works.

As you paddle towards Chelsea Harbour, look out for the brass ball atop Belvedere Tower. It rises and falls with the tide. Here and throughout the passage upstream, stay out of the main navigation channel. The reason becomes evident when a high-speed Thames Clipper zooms past in the fairway, creating a massive wake. Rebranded as Uber Boats, these commuter boats zip in and out of the Chelsea Harbour pier ahead and continue with stops at St Mary's Wandsworth Pier, Wandsworth Riverside Quarter and

BELOW Leave Wandsworth Bridge behind.

ABOVE A magical night paddle by Albert Bridge with fireworks over the Thames.

Putney, running all day, seven days a week. When possible, pass behind piers and use the bridge arches closest to shore.

The first bridge, Battersea Rail Bridge, carries London Overground trains. Next is Wandsworth Bridge, and soon after you may hear the random roar of a helicopter overhead – this is the London Heliport in Battersea. The containers upstream of Wandsworth Bridge are waiting to be filled with waste and transported by barges downstream to Bexley to generate energy. The River Wandle also flows into the Thames here, but is sadly too shallow to paddle.

Further upstream, on the opposite bank, is the Hurlingham Club, London's only country club, with extensive riverside grounds and a famously closed waiting list.

Paddling under Fulham Railway Bridge, you soon reach Putney. Originally called Fulham Bridge, Putney Bridge is one of the few in London with a church at each end – All Saints in Fulham and St Mary's in Putney. The embankment here is lively with rowing clubs, so stay to the right for a close-up view of Craven Cottage stadium.

Continue under Hammersmith Bridge, the halfway point, and paddle through Barnes, Mortlake and Chiswick to finish at Active360's base at Kew Bridge Arches. An epic London paddle. For more details on the Putney to Kew stretch, see route 13.

Linking routes

- 12 Kew Bridge to Richmond
- 13 Putney to Kew Bridge
- 15 Battersea to Greenwich

ABOVE Paddling towards Chiswick Bridge.

ABOVE The exit point is a public slipway next to Kew Bridge arches.

Wildlife highlight

Muddy waters – turbidity
Don't judge the Thames by its brown colour. Twice a day without fail, the tide rolls in and out, stirring up sediment from the riverbed. This constant tidal movement keeps tiny particles of mud, silt and organic matter suspended in the water, giving it the signature murky colour. This turbidity is perfectly natural and a good thing. Those particles carry nutrients that sustain a diverse ecosystem. Over 125 fish species, a few marine mammals and numerous birds thrive here, all supported by the nutrient-rich habitat that many mistake for simply dirty water.

Tuck in

Off-the-water stops are not recommended between Chelsea and Putney Bridge.
Along the route upstream of Putney Bridge: The Clubhouse, The Crabtree, The Blue Boat, The Blue Anchor, The Dove, Black Lion, Old Ship, The Watermans Arms, White Hart, The Ship, Bulls Head, The City Barge, The Bell & Crown, The Steam Packet.
Kew Bridge: One Over the Ait, The Express Tavern, Strand Cafe, The Roastery.

Paddle providers

- **Active360** – active360.co.uk
- **London Sports Trust Blades** – londonsportstrust.org

NEED TO KNOW

■ The Port of London Authority (PLA) manages the Thames Tideway below Teddington Lock. This section is challenging, with a fast-flowing tide and fixed obstructions like bridges and piers increasing the risks. The Tideway Code restricts paddling below Putney Bridge, where the tidal Thames becomes Britain's busiest waterway – large commercial and high-speed vessels adding extra hazards. Find the Code on the PLA website.

■ Specific restrictions apply for paddling, especially SUP, below Putney Bridge. This area is best explored with an organised tour. There is no public launch from the London Sports Trust's site at Cremorne Riverside Centre.

■ This route is for experienced paddlers only. Do not paddle alone. Understanding tides and river flow is crucial for safety. Paddle only when the river is not in flood or high flow.

■ At least one person must carry a VHF radio – London Vessel Traffic Services (VTS), VHF channel 14.

■ In this section between Putney and Syon Reach, paddle against the tide by 'working the slacks' and using slower water on the inside of bends.

15 BATTERSEA TO GREENWICH

Book ahead! **Ideal for Londoners, visitors and tourists**, this all-inclusive kayak tour from Battersea to Greenwich is a must-do. The busy, fast-flowing stretch of Central London is restricted for paddlers, especially paddleboarders. A guided tour is the safest way to explore it. See London's major landmarks from the perspective of a kayak, with the guide sharing stories that bring the city's history and current affairs to life.

The Lowdown

DIFFICULTY ●●●●
WATER TYPE Tidal river
LAUNCH/EXIT Foreshore
DISTANCE 18km (one way)
PORTAGES 0
LICENCE REQUIRED? No, but restricted

START
- ///scrap.museum.hello
- Clapham Junction (District Line, Piccadilly Line, Mildmay, Windrush, National Rail) – 15-min walk
- Check parking apps

FINISH
- ///sock.stem.homes
- North Greenwich (Jubilee, Cable Car) – 20-min walk
- North Greenwich Station Car Park, 5 Millennium Way, London SE10 0PH, height restriction 1.9m – 15-min walk

A brief history

London's story began with the Romans. They established what would become London along the Thames around AD 50. Back then, the river was gentler, wider and shallower. It was lined with tidal creeks, marshland and mudflats. The land on the north bank was more stable, suitable for mooring and construction. Originally, the city developed there.

Over centuries, the natural river was engineered for urban expansion, defence,

RIGHT Battersea launch spot.

LEFT Albert Bridge on the way downstream.

RIGHT Kayaking past the iconic Battersea Power Station.

maritime trade and flood control. As London grew, land was reclaimed from the Thames. The river was made straighter and narrower. The soft edges were replaced with river walls and embankments, squeezing the river into a tight channel. Large ships required deeper waters, so the riverbed was dredged. All these alterations resulted in the river running faster and fiercer. The flow is at its peak between Battersea and Tower Bridge, the narrowest stretch. Structures like the many bridges, piers and moorings further increase the speed and create obstruction for the natural forces, both stream and wind.

The Port of London Authority (PLA), established in 1909, manages the tidal Thames from Teddington Lock to the North Sea. Central London is a restricted, high-risk paddle zone due to fast flow, heavy commercial traffic and limited exit points.

The paddle It must be every paddler's dream to glide past the Houses of Parliament and all of London's landmarks. But it turns out that paddling the Thames through Central London is mostly off-limits, especially for paddleboarders. The easiest and safest way to tick off this London classic is by joining an organised kayak tour. The London Kayak Company (LKC), led by Harry Whelan, has been guiding paddlers through this fast-moving, high-traffic section since 1996.

The LKC website declares 'see London as never before'. Their Kayak Bus offers a one-way trip from Battersea to Greenwich. Or the other way around. For London all lit up, opt for the Night Bus. The tours are adults-only and 100 per cent for sightseeing, powered by your paddling. Double kayaks with rudders are used. The rear paddler is responsible for steering, the rudder controlled by foot pedals.

In West London, the meeting point is by the riverside at St Mary's Church in Battersea, across from Cheyne Walk in Chelsea (see route 14). The process is simple – sign a waiver and get kitted out with waterproofs, buoyancy aid and a paddle. Valuables, including phones, are stashed inside the kayak for storage. Guides take photos, so no need to fuss with a phone on the water. Then, hop into a kayak. Final adjustments are made and the group is off, shepherded by two guides in agile singles.

The paddle downstream starts unfolding in a leisurely rhythm, one bridge at a time. 'Slow down, slow down', the guide tells eager paddlers. The group stays tight for visibility, but transits are swift, taken in turns. Bridge arches are numbered from the north bank, starting with arch #1. Before each bridge, the guide gives instructions on which arch to take and what to aim for. No guesswork, just follow the directions.

Battersea Bridge is the first of the 17 crossings. Under all the Central London bridges, the river pushes back against its confinement through the gaps between buttresses, swirling with eddies, currents and turbulence. The key? To keep paddling, because without momentum, steering becomes impossible.

Modern residential developments line the Battersea side. The Chelsea Embankment opposite is a sharp contrast, with its old-London charm. To appreciate the beauty of Albert Bridge ahead, you

ABOVE Big Ben and the Houses of Parliament.

have to see it fully illuminated at night. The original tollbooths remain.

Paddle past Battersea Park, where Buddha watches over the river from the Peace Pagoda. A few bridges later, you'll see Battersea Power Station. Once the UK's largest power station, it is now a new retail, residential and office destination. After Chelsea Bridge, you are in the Heart of London in PLA terms.

The piers of the Uber Boat by Thames Clippers also appear at regular intervals, 16 along this route. The high-speed river boats are quickly in and out, kicking up a massive wake. RIBs race past in showers of spray. Luckily, the guides stay tuned to London Vessel Traffic Services (VTS) on VHF radio, keeping tabs on river traffic.

James Bond fans will recognise MI6 by Vauxhall Bridge, headquarters of the British Secret Intelligence Service. Exclusion Zone applies in front of it, same as the Houses of Parliament, both off-limits for security. Want the view forever? A one-bed at Riverwalk on Millbank will set you back £1 million, concierge service included.

Between the bridges, a succession of familiar London landmarks rolls past, but from a whole new angle, low on the water with waves lapping around. It feels almost unreal. Past Lambeth Bridge, the Palace of Westminster appears ahead, home to the UK Parliament. Love it or not, the Gothic Revival style building is unmistakable. The guides pull the group together, right on cue. Big Ben chimes and everyone gets their shot with the unique backdrop. Without the river, none of this would be here.

With heavy river traffic, the waters turn rough between Westminster and Hungerford Bridges and there are proper waves. The natural tidal set wants to push the kayaks off course and with the busy Waterloo Pier downstream of Westminster Bridge, positioning is key. But the guide has it covered. Clear and snappy, or colourful if you are not paying attention, his instructions keep everyone on track, allowing paddlers to take in the sights. And

ABOVE Tower Bridge is another iconic backdrop.

there it is: the London Eye, turning slowly. Once called the Millennium Wheel, it was meant to be temporary but has now stood for 25 years.

Across from Charing Cross and Temple, the South Bank stretches out on both sides of Waterloo Bridge, a riverside packed with culture, theatre and live performances. The OXO Tower glows in the distance. In the 1920s, designers dodged a skyline advertising ban by working two circles and a cross into the tower's windows. Just a happy coincidence, apparently. Below, at low tide, the foreshore reveals a sandy patch known as Ernie's Beach.

Paddling under Blackfriars Road and Railway bridges, St Paul's Cathedral appears on the left with the City of London rising beside it, featuring the Walkie Talkie, Cheesegrater and Gherkin. It is a contrast of old and new. London's skyline is unique, partly due to an urban planning policy from the 1930s, 'St Paul's Height', which limits high-rise buildings that could block the view of St Paul's and other historic landmarks.

The steady rhythm of paddles hitting the water is almost hypnotic. London drifts past like an old film reel, unspooling scene by scene. The Millennium Bridge crosses from St Paul's to another repurposed power station, now Tate Modern. It was the first new bridge over the Thames in London in more than a century, built just for foot traffic.

There have been several London Bridges between the City of London and Southwark since Roman times. The current uninspiring crossing dates from the 1970s. Beyond the nursery rhyme, you may recognise it as the reference point for tide tables. London Bridge also marks the beginning of the Pool of London, which extends to Limehouse. It was once the busiest port in the world, and a wall of wharves.

You only appreciate the sheer size of HMS *Belfast* when paddling right past it. Behind, The Shard pierces the southern skyline, but it is Tower Bridge that steals the show, its neo-Gothic style matching the

ABOVE The *Cutty Sark*.

RIGHT Prospect of Whitby pub, Execution Dock.

OPPOSITE The Royal Naval College.

Tower of London. Queen Victoria did not want the new bridge to outshine the Tower. The bascules still lift around 1,000 times a year, now at the push of a button. The final bridge on this route is the perfect spot for another photo, halfway through the tour. There are two more Victorian crossings further east, but they are underground, the foot tunnels of Greenwich and Woolwich.

The PLA defines the Thames below Tower Bridge as Lower Tideway. Here, between Wapping and Shadwell to the north and Bermondsey and Rotherhithe to the south, the river widens and meanders. Going around the top of the Rotherhithe peninsula, the entrance to Limehouse Basin (see route 28) appears on the left with Antony Gormley's sculpture on the foreshore. But it is the gleaming skyscrapers of Canary Wharf that take the limelight. Originally built as enclosed docks to ease congestion and curb theft on the river, the area reinvented itself as a high-rise financial district.

The last stretch of the route loops around the Isle of Dogs. Famous for setting the world's clocks, Greenwich is on the opposite side. You paddle past the *Cutty Sark*, one of Britain's most celebrated sea-going vessels, and finally, the Old Royal Naval College. Three hours after launching, you land, buzzing, on a Greenwich beach. An iconic London paddle completed.

Linking route

- 14 Chelsea to Kew

Wildlife highlight

Harbour porpoise (*Phocoena phocoena*) Dolphins in the Thames? Not quite. Harbour porpoises are small, shy cetaceans, more closely related to whales. Recent studies have used acoustic detection to track them and the Thames Estuary has proven an important habitat. Occasionally, they venture up the Tideway. Unlike dolphins,

they do not leap but surface with a gentle roll, their small triangular dorsal fins slicing the water. They navigate and find their prey using echolocation, producing high-pitched clicks to sense their surroundings. But with such sensitive hearing, they are easily disturbed by noise from boat traffic and construction.

Tuck in

- Make sure you are well fuelled for the Central London paddle adventure, because there is no way to get off the water along the route.
- In Battersea, you will find a few cafes at Battersea Square, and in Greenwich there are several options in and around North Greenwich Tube station.

Paddle provider

- London Kayak Company – londonkayakcompany.com

NEED TO KNOW

■ The Port of London Authority (PLA) manages the Thames Tideway below Teddington Lock. This section of the river in Central London is challenging due to fast-flowing tide, heavy commercial traffic and fixed obstructions like bridges and piers. Paddling, especially SUP, is restricted below Putney Bridge. For up-to-date guidelines, refer to the Tideway Code on the PLA website.

■ Unless you are very experienced and meet the Tideway Code criteria, it is recommended to explore this route with an organised tour.

■ At least one person must carry a VHF radio – London Vessel Traffic Services (VTS), VHF channel 14 – and contact VTS before navigation.

CANALS

The historic canal network that was engineered as the Industrial Revolution's mass transport system has retired into a life of leisure. The old working waterways are now perfect for mindful exploration by paddled craft.

The following collection of 18 routes covers 137km of London's main canals and navigations, a crash course in canal geography. In winter, when your phone is pinging with river flow rate and flood warning notifications, take your pick here: The Grand Union Canal takes you from the Colne Valley down to Brentford, with its Paddington Arm stretching from Hayes to Little Venice and its Slough Arm, well, leading to Slough. The Regent's Canal winds past Regent's Park, Camden, King's Cross and Hackney before joining the Thames at Limehouse. From there, the aptly named Limehouse Cut offers a shortcut to the Lee Navigation, which heads north to Hertford along the canalised River Lea. Completing the network, the Hertford Union Canal links the Lee Navigation to the Regent's Canal.

ABOVE Permanent moorings along the Slough Arm of the Grand Union Canal.

ABOVE At Coal Drops Yard along Regent's Canal.

If you are still holding on to the notion of London's urban canals as murky, stagnant ditches, it is time for a fresh outlook. Sure, they are not all scenic and some stretches are gritty, worn by industry and time, but that is part of their charm. These canals proudly carry traces of their industrial character, but regeneration has transformed much of the network. And change is constant. It is the contrasts that make urban paddling here so compelling – nature and cityscape, old and new, tranquillity and traffic. Even in the heart of London, you will find patches of wilderness.

Along the way, you are likely to pick up some canal lingo, learn to tell a coot from a moorhen and, without a doubt, become an expert at portaging. More than anything, you will see London from a whole new perspective – one where time slows, the water stills and the capital's diverse neighbourhoods unfold in a way you have never seen before.

Planning

All waterways in this section are managed by the Canal & River Trust (CRT). Locks and tunnels require portaging, so plan accordingly. Check the CRT website for closures, works or events affecting your route. Winter maintenance schedules are published in advance and you can set up alerts for updates at canalrivertrust.org.uk.

16 RICKMANSWORTH TO WATFORD GRAND UNION

Escape the city. Technically in Hertfordshire, but connected to London on the Metropolitan Line, Rickmansworth along the Grand Union Canal offers excellent rural paddling within the M25. This 9km round trip from Rickmansworth to the outskirts of Watford and back is surrounded by lakes, rivers and nature reserves. Classic canal-side charm, canal boats, lock keepers' cottages and bridges with strong ties to the waterway's industrial history. Plus, free parking is always a win.

The Lowdown

DIFFICULTY 💧

WATER TYPE Canal

LAUNCH/EXIT Towpath

DISTANCE 9km (round trip)

PORTAGES 3 x 2 (Locks: Batchworth, Lot Mead, Common Moor)

LICENCE REQUIRED? Yes

START/FINISH
- ///harp.coast.above
- Rickmansworth (Metropolitan Line, National Rail) – 15-min walk
- Rickmansworth Aquadrome Car Park, Frogmoor Lane, Three Rivers WD3 1NB – free

A brief history

Paddled craft are the newcomers on British canals, originally built for transporting goods. Early canal boats evolved to fit the narrow locks. The boats are typically 6 feet 10 inches wide and up to 70 feet long. The boats were wooden and towed by horses, mules or donkeys, which explains the towpath running alongside the canal. In the 20th century, steam and later diesel engines replaced horse power and boats were built from steel and iron. Boats sometimes operated in pairs, the towed boat called a butty, from the word buddy.

A barge is anything wider than a narrowboat, and are often cargo-carrying. Some leisure craft are referred to as wide beams and a Dutch barge fits in this category, too. Houseboats are simply moored homes, many unable to move under their own power.

The Batchworth Lock Canal Centre along this route used to be an overnight stop for narrowboats carrying freight between London and the Midlands, with stables and pubs. Here you can meet *Roger*, a rare, fully restored wooden

CANALS

ABOVE The first hints of autumn colour along the canal.

motorised narrowboat. Built in 1936 to transport coal while towing its butty, *Daphne*, *Roger* is now maintained by the Rickmansworth Waterways Trust, upholding the legacy of working boats on the Grand Union Canal.

The paddle
This route starts at Rickmansworth Aquadrome, a nature reserve in Hertfordshire with a free car park right by the canal. Another bonus feature, there is a public toilet in the park. The four lakes here were created by gravel extraction, some of which helped build Wembley Stadium. Unfortunately, use of the lakes is reserved for local clubs only, so head for the Grand Union Canal. Put in from the towpath and paddle upstream to pass Bridge No 174. Wave hello to the folks at DavePaddles. If you need any last-minute supplies, there is a Tesco superstore with mooring spots and all.

WATFORD

CROXLEY GREEN

CROXLEY

Lock 79 Common Moor

Lock 80 Lot Mead

RICKMANSWORTH

Lock 81 Batchworth

Start
Finish

PADDLE LONDON

LEFT Pumping up the boards. Are you team manual or electric?

BELOW Every canal is an invitation to explore.

OPPOSITE Feels like the countryside.

Rickmansworth is a confluence of three rivers – the Colne, Chess and Gade. The first one you encounter is the River Colne when it crosses the canal, entering on your left and exiting onto your right. Ignore it and continue straight, taking care as the area can be busy with boats. Pass carefully under Bridge No 173 to arrive at the Batchworth Lock Canal Centre, home to Rickmansworth Waterways. Worth a stop when you get off the water to portage at Batchworth Lock (No 81). And the cakes at Café@Lock 81 are always tempting. The channel on the left leads to the River Chess and Lock No 81A, but stay on the Grand Union. Once back on the water, follow the curve of the canal, paddle past the weirs and the Colne backwaters on the right. The canal and river are joined here.

The next stretch is peaceful and green. Croxley and Broadacres lakes on the left are mostly hidden from view, parkland and wetlands lining the waterway on the right. The Colne splits up from the canal and the River Gade parts to the right, but it keeps reappearing throughout the journey. Portage at Lot Mead Lock (No 80), just a pylon and a cargo train bridge breaking the timeless idyll of the tidily kept gardens of the lock keeper's cottage.

Paddle through the ancient woodland and moorland surrounding the canal. During the summer, you may even come across cattle grazing at the Croxley Common

Moor nature reserve. The final portage on the upstream stretch is at Common Moor Lock (No 79). Keep paddling until you pass Bridgewater Basin on your right. The Metropolitan Line bridge No 168A marks your turnaround point. Enjoy a break at the canal-side before retracing your strokes back downstream to Rickmansworth Aquadrome. If time permits, explore Salters Cut, the canalised section of River Chess, from the Batchworth Lock Canal Centre past Lock No 81A.

Linking route
- 17 Rickmansworth to Uxbridge (Grand Union)

Wildlife highlight
Conservation grazing
Croxley Common Moor, a 40-hectare nature reserve between the Grand Union Canal and River Gade, is a designated Site of Special Scientific Interest (SSSI). Its historic grassland is carefully maintained through conservation grazing: 30 cows are released to roam the moor from June to October, munching on coarse grasses. This traditional method helps wildflowers thrive, supporting insects, aiding pollination and creating more food for birds while preserving the moor's unique biodiversity.

Tuck in
- **Rickmansworth**: Several pubs and cafes in Rickmansworth, The Cafe in the Park at launch.
- **Along the route**, Tesco, The White Bear, Café@Lock 81.

Paddle providers
- **DavePaddles** – davepaddles.co.uk
- **Bury Lake Young Mariners** – blym.org.uk

NEED TO KNOW

■ The Canal & River Trust is the navigation authority on the Grand Union Canal. A small craft licence is required, also covered by Paddle UK membership.

■ Follow the navigation rules and keep to the right-hand side in the direction of travel. There can be quite a bit of traffic.

■ Avoid Rickmansworth Aquadrome car park on Saturday mornings during Parkrun, it gets very busy. Arrive either well before or after.

■ Personal paddle craft are not allowed on Aquadrome lakes. All watersports must go through the on-site clubs.

17 RICKMANSWORTH TO UXBRIDGE GRAND UNION

This 10km paddle from Rickmansworth to Uxbridge follows the Grand Union Canal's mainline, crossing from Hertfordshire into Greater London. The route cuts through the green and blue Colne Valley, unique due to the grid of lakes and rivers mingling with the canal all the way. Expect a spooky abandoned industrial site, scenic lock keepers' cottages and a contrast of old and new – from 19th-century canal engineering to the new HS2 Viaduct. Six portages may test your fitness, but the scenery more than makes up for it.

A brief history

The past and future of transport come together along this stretch. In the late 18th century, the Grand Junction Canal was dug to link Birmingham and London. After the waterway became part of the Grand Union Canal network, it was proudly advertised that a canal boat journey transporting goods could be completed in 50 hours by travelling day and night. Now, the high-speed railway HS2 will connect the two cities once more, achieving the 220km distance in 49 minutes.

This paddle route offers a unique view of the HS2 Colne Valley Viaduct as it extends over the Grand Union Canal in Denham. The UK's longest rail bridge now crosses the country's longest canal – both massive engineering projects that sparked debate in their time.

The paddle

The Rickmansworth Aquadrome along the main arm of the Grand Union Canal is a brilliant start point for a paddle. Close to the station, there is also a free car park, public toilet and café in the nature reserve. Find a safe gap between boats to put in your craft and launch downstream to your right, away from Batchworth Lock Canal Centre.

This route travels through the Colne Valley countryside from Rickmansworth to Uxbridge. You pass along green spaces,

ABOVE Passing under the HS2 Colne Valley Viaduct.

ABOVE Surrounded by Colne Valley greenery.

The Lowdown

DIFFICULTY 💧

WATER TYPE Canal

LAUNCH/EXIT Towpath

DISTANCE 8.5–10km (one way)

PORTAGES 6 (Locks: Stockers, Springwell, Copper Mill, Black Jack's, Widewater, Denham Deep)

LICENCE REQUIRED? Yes

START
- ///harp.coast.above
- Rickmansworth (Metropolitan Line, National Rail) – 15-min walk
- Rickmansworth Aquadrome Car Park, Frogmoor Lane, Three Rivers WD3 1NB – free

FINISH
- ///radio.deals.guard (1)
- ///tester.bags.vine (2)
- Uxbridge (1) (Metropolitan Line, Piccadilly Line) – 15-min walk
- Colne Valley Regional Park Visitor Centre car park (2), Denham Court Drive, Denham, UB9 5PG – 5-min walk

RICKMANSWORTH
Lock 82 Stockers Lock — Start
Lock 83 Springwell Lock
Lock 84 Coppermill Lock
HAREFIELD
Lock 85 Black Jack's Lock
Lock 86 Widewater
Lock 87 Denham Deep Lock
Finish
UXBRIDGE

woodland and endless stretches of water. Stay inside the neat banks of the canal throughout, although the park's 60 lakes and 5 rivers are tempting as they intermingle with the Grand Union.

Portage at Stockers Lock (No 82) with its postcard-perfect lock keeper's cottage. Coal boats used to pay tolls here en route to London. Just beyond is Stockers Farm, which you may recognise from films or TV. Paddle a short stretch to arrive at one of London's eeriest waterway landmarks: the abandoned Harefield Limeworks, nicknamed the Hanging Monkey for the giant stuffed monkey dangling from its derelict heights.

Next up are Springwell Lock (No 83) and Copper Mill Lock (No 84). Nearby, the Maple Cross sewage works, nicknamed by boaters as the Stink Hole, brings you back to urban reality. The River Colne flows in parallel, mingling with the canal now and then, while model planes buzz overhead. If you have paddled around Paddington and Little Venice, you may spot some familiar hulls: tugs, barges and hoppers from Wood Hall & Heward's hire fleet.

Keep away from the fierce currents at the Copper Mill weir exit on your left before Bridge No 177. The kayak slalom course is best left to the pros, but it is entertaining watching kayakers race through the gates. The Coy Carp pub sits between the canal and river here, overlooking the Pynesfield lakes on the other side.

Black Jack's Lock (No 85) greets you with its old thatched cottage. Portage and enjoy a change in scenery as a grassy slope rises to your left. At the top, the white Old Orchard pub offers what must be stunning views of the canal, lakes and countryside, if you're up for the climb.

Another portage at Widewater Lock (No 86) and you have reached 6km. Then paddle past The River Garden and Harefield Marina. The greenery begins to give way to signs of the city – some fly-tipping and tired moorings. Above, the sleek structure of

HS2 Colne Valley Viaduct slices through the sky, linking two cities and eras. After that, the Denham railway viaduct feels rather understated.

Follow the waterway and pylons to Denham Deep Lock (No 87), the heavyweight champion of the Grand Union Canal with a 3.5m drop, the deepest on the network. Like all the locks on the mainline, it is a double-wide design, able to handle 70-ton barges. Here, the Colne, Misbourne and Fray's rivers converge. The nearby Colne Valley Regional Park Visitor Centre offers a café, car park, toilets and more information about the area.

In under 2km, you arrive at the final destination of this route. Welcome to the West London suburb of Uxbridge. Take out at Uxbridge Lock (No 88) and cross over to the right-hand side. The towpath leads you to the Swan & Bottle pub – a nice spot to celebrate the end of the adventure, just a five-minute walk away.

Linking route

- 16 Rickmansworth to Watford (Grand Union)

LEFT Floating pennywort taking over the canal.

RIGHT Stockers Farm, a popular filming location.

Wildlife highlight

Common reed (*Phragmites australis*) Reed beds are wetland habitats dominated by the common reed. Springwell Reedbed next to the canal in Colne Valley is the largest in London. Covering 3 hectares, it accounts for 6 per cent of the capital's reed beds. Reed beds are essential ecosystems, especially in built-up areas, because they support wildlife, birds, invertebrates and mammals. But they don't stop there – reed beds also work hard behind the scenes, filtering pollutants, oxygenating water and helping manage flood risk. With a shortage of these natural filters in urban areas, floating reed beds have been popping up on London's waterways. A simple solution with big benefits.

Tuck in

- **Rickmansworth**: Several pubs and cafés in Rickmansworth, The Cafe in the Park at launch.
- **Along the route**: Coy Carp and The River Garden.
- **Uxbridge**: Swan & Bottle.

Paddle providers

- **DavePaddles** – davepaddles.co.uk
- **Bury Lake Young Mariners** – blym.org.uk

NEED TO KNOW

■ The Canal & River Trust is the navigation authority on the Grand Union Canal. A small craft licence is required, also covered by Paddle UK membership.

■ Follow the navigation rules and keep to the right-hand side in the direction of travel. During summer, it tends to be hectic on the water.

■ Avoid Rickmansworth Aquadrome car park on Saturday mornings during Parkrun, it is busy. Arrive either well before or after.

■ Personal paddle craft are not allowed on Aquadrome lakes. All watersports must go through the on-site clubs.

18 WEST DRAYTON TO SLOUGH GRAND UNION

For an off-the-beaten-paddle adventure, head to the Slough Arm of the Grand Union Canal. This 9km, lock-free stretch from West Drayton in London to the unsung town of Slough in Berkshire is an often overlooked gem of peaceful waters and minimal boat traffic. None of the typical landmarks, but count on abundant wildlife, characterful narrowboat moorings, chats with anglers and the occasional battle with stubborn reeds and weeds. Surrounded by the lush Colne Valley, this route highlights why Hillingdon is one of the greenest boroughs in the UK.

The Lowdown

DIFFICULTY

WATER TYPE Canal

LAUNCH/EXIT Towpath

DISTANCE 9km (one way)

PORTAGES 0

LICENCE REQUIRED? Yes

START
- ///tops.manliness.piano
- West Drayton (Elizabeth Line, National Rail) – 5-min walk
- Brandville Road Car Park, Brandville Rd, West Drayton UB7 7LT, height restriction 2m – 10-min walk

FINISH
- ///author.shop.shed
- Slough (Elizabeth Line, National Rail) – 10-min walk
- Slough Station – East, Brunel Way, Slough SL1 1XW, height restriction 2.6m – 10 min

ABOVE The station, through the fence, is very conveniently located to the water.

CANALS

ABOVE *Bob's your Uncle.*

ABOVE *Father and son fishing.*

A brief history

The Slough Arm was a latecomer to the canal era. One of the last canals in Britain, it opened in 1882 as an 8km branch of the Grand Union Canal. After earlier disputes with millers in the area, three aqueducts were included in the design to ensure no one would run out of water. Built to serve Slough's brick-making industry, the canal reached its peak in 1905. It moved 192,000 tons of cargo – bricks for London's construction needs and, not to return empty, rubbish from London to backfill the pits. Quite the deal. But by the mid-20th century, resources had depleted and commercial traffic dried up. A plan in the 1960s to replace the canal with a road hit a wall of local opposition and in 1975 the arm reopened for leisure.

In the early 2000s, Slough gained infamy as the setting for Ricky Gervais's TV series 'The Office'. In 2024, it was named the most miserable place to live in the UK. As a branch terminus, the town sees so few visiting boats that it is on the Inland Waterways Association's 'Cruise it or lose it' list. On the water, Slough's story changes – the canal is peaceful, green and ideal for a quiet escape.

The paddle

The Elizabeth Line provides quick access to West Drayton in the London Borough of Hillingdon. You may be lucky enough to get onto the water right in front of the station, if the gate is open to the car park designated for Ashley Court residents. If not, cross the Yiewsley High Street Bridge (No 192), walk down the stairs to access the

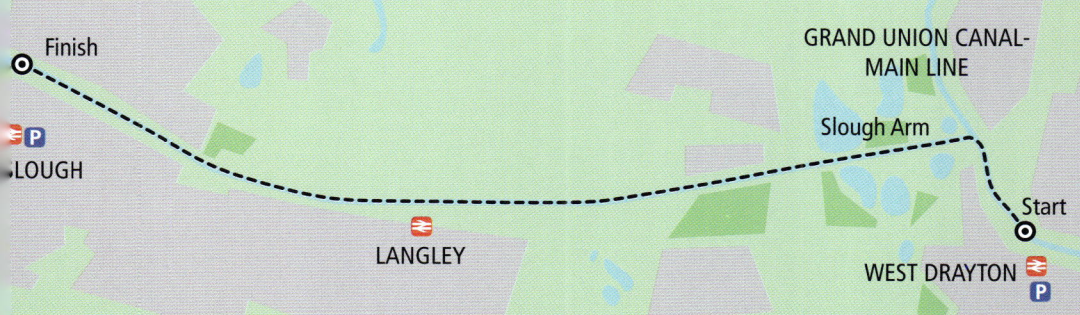

Grand Union Canal towpath and begin your upstream journey.

On the mainline section, paddle through the suburban edge of London, with housing developments, narrowboat moorings and the occasional industrial estate. Overgrown greenery softens the edges. There is a Tesco superstore right by the canal for any last-minute supplies. The first aqueduct passes over the River Pinn so understatedly that if you blink, you may miss it. Paddle straight to Cowley Peachey Junction, then turn left under the iron footbridge onto the Slough Arm.

The Slough branch is an unassuming waterway into Slough Basin. Surprisingly, the first bridge is numbered zero, the footbridge leading to the Packet Boat Marina. Some industrial structures and pylons crop up, of course, but the mood on the water is peaceful, anglers quietly casting their lines. Cross an aqueduct over Fray's River, one of three cast-iron aqueducts in quick succession – another rarity in the UK canal network. Keep an eye out for Second World War defences like pillboxes along the way.

Follow the route under the M25, the roar of traffic momentarily clashing with the peaceful waterway. A massive advertising screen looms above, targeting the M25 commuters. Did they realise canal-goers would see it too? Soon, you reach High Line Yachting in Iver, a boatyard with two-abreast moorings, storage and curious liveaboards. The channel gets increasingly overgrown with weed and silt. Not easily navigable for boats, make your way through a verdant tunnel.

The railway runs alongside as you approach Slough's outskirts, paddling past houses and parks. Finally, the canal ends unceremoniously at Slough Basin. Redevelopment is on the way, but for now it is more grit than glam. Slough rail station is not far, with the Elizabeth Line zipping you to Paddington in just 30 minutes.

Linking route
- 17 Rickmansworth to Uxbridge (Grand Union)

Wildlife highlight
Moorhen (*Gallinula chloropus*) and **Coot** (*Fulica atra*)
Can you tell moorhens and coots apart? Close relatives, both waterbirds are familiar sights on London's canals. Coots are larger, with all-black plumage and a white facial shield, while moorhens are smaller and more timid, also blackish but with red-and-yellow beaks. In short, identification by beak colour: 'CooT whiTe and MooRhen Red'. It actually works. And their chicks? The cute fluffy balls with orange and red heads you see between April and July are coots. Coots swim boldly in open water, whereas moorhens prefer to hug the edges, hiding among reeds and vegetation. Perhaps that is why you see so many moorhens on the Slough Arm.

ABOVE Some of the navigation is very overgrown.

LEFT Paddling through West Drayton.

Tuck in
- **West Drayton**: Bean There Drank That! café.
- **Along the route**: Tesco.
- **Slough**: There are several cafés around Slough station to get your coffee fix. Perk coffee cart is a local favourite but closed on weekends.

NEED TO KNOW
■ The Canal & River Trust is the navigation authority on the Grand Union Canal, also the Slough Arm. A small craft licence is required, also covered by Paddle UK membership.

19 HAYES TO HANWELL GRAND UNION

This one-way paddle takes you from Hayes on the main line of the Grand Union Canal, passing through Southall, North Hyde and Norwood Green, to Hanwell. The route starts in an industrial area but soon transitions to more suburban and even rural landscapes. History lovers are treated to two Scheduled Monuments along the way: Three Bridges and Hanwell Flight of Locks. At just 6km, the distance is manageable, but the eight portages add an extra challenge to the paddle.

The Lowdown

DIFFICULTY

WATER TYPE Canal

LAUNCH/EXIT Towpath

DISTANCE 6km (one way)

PORTAGES 8 (Locks: Norwood Top, Norwood, Hanwell Flight of Locks)

LICENCE REQUIRED? Yes

START
- ///spits.crib.payer
- Hayes & Harlington (Elizabeth Line) – 5-min walk
- Hayes & Harlington Station Car Park, Viveash Close, Hayes and Harlington UB3 4BX – 5-min walk

FINISH
- ///opera.chart.snaps
- Hanwell (Elizabeth Line) – 20-min walk
- George Street Car Park, George St, London W7 3TA – 15-min walk

A brief history

The Grand Union Canal was originally called the Grand Junction Canal, a name still seen on some bridges along the route. Notice all the mileposts pointing to Braunston? It was a key junction where the Grand Junction met the Oxford Canal, connecting Birmingham to London. In the canal's heyday, these mileposts helped canal companies calculate tolls based on distance travelled and weight of cargo. The Grand Union, as we know it today, took shape in the 1920s, when several waterways, including the Grand Junction, merged into one.

ABOVE Three Bridges is a scheduled monument.

CANALS

LEFT Lock keeper's cottage on the Hanwell Flight of Locks.

There are two Scheduled Monuments in Hanwell: Three Bridges and the Hanwell Flight of Locks, both of which share similar legal protection to Stonehenge. Three Bridges, designed by Isambard Kingdom Brunel, is a unique three-tiered junction with road above canal above rail. A road bridge, a canal aqueduct and a railway cutting intersect on three levels. Try to figure out which came first.

Just downstream, the Hanwell Flight of Locks is another achievement of late 18th-century engineering. London's largest lock system consists of six locks that lower the canal by 16 metres over less than a kilometre, running alongside the high Victorian security wall of the former County Asylum. The flight was once one of the busiest in the country, with narrowboats and barges navigating the locks on their way to and from the industrial North, Midlands' manufacturing centres and London.

The paddle

The Elizabeth Line makes it easy to get to Hayes in no time from Central London, with step-free access – ideal for transporting paddle kit. For those driving, there is a car park at Hayes & Harlington station. From there, head down Station Road, cross the bridge and take the stairs down to the towpath. Launch downstream on the main branch of the Grand Union Canal, leaving Bridge No 200 behind.

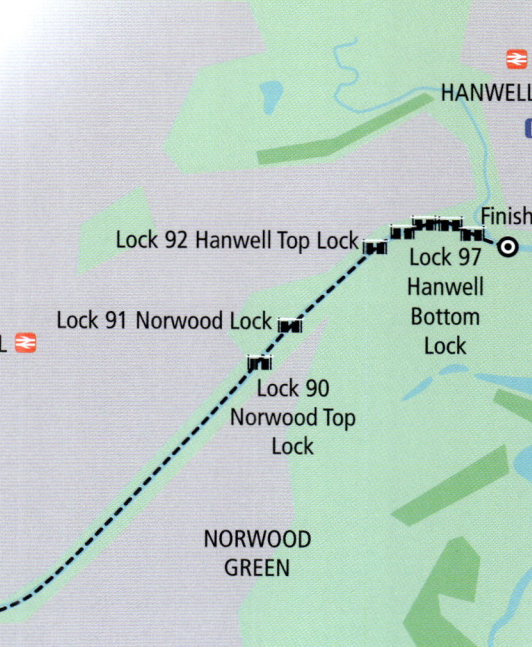

Paddle along canal-side that is rapidly changing, with former industrial areas giving way to new developments. Just before Bridge No 200E, you pass over an aqueduct. It is the River Crane, meandering its way to the Thames at Isleworth (see route 12).

A kilometre in, by the big supermarket, the Paddington Arm branches off to the left, running over 20km to Paddington Basin (see route 23). Stay on the main line, continuing east with Southall on the left and North Hyde and Norwood Green on the right. One of the old mileposts appears shortly after Bull's Bridge: 'Braunston 88 miles'. Good thing you are going the other way.

Past the halfway point after Bridge No 203A footbridge, Havelock Road Arm appears on the left. Known as Maypole Dock, this almost kilometre-long private canal used to serve the Quaker Oats factory, now replaced by a residential tower block.

The first two locks on this route ease you into the Hanwell descent. Portage at Norwood Top Lock (No 90) and carry on down. Glade Lane Canalside Park lines the left bank around Norwood Lock (No 91), with nature conservation zones and a sustainable drainage system. Just past the park, the Three Bridges reserve on the opposite side has been taken over by Canada geese, so be prepared for droppings if you stop to view the info boards.

Paddle under Windmill Lane Bridge, better known as Three Bridges, Isambard Kingdom Brunel's triple-decker structure, where road,

ABOVE Portaging along the flight of locks.

BELOW Egyptian goose with its young.

canal and railway meet. From a paddler's perspective, you can really appreciate one of Brunel's last projects: the road up top, the canal in the middle and the railway in a deep cutting below.

What is your preferred portage style? Plenty of time to practise on the final just under a kilometre's distance to carry the kit down the Hanwell Flight of Locks, a series of six locks (Nos 92–97). If it is any consolation, it is still faster than boats moving down the locks. On a good day, it takes them more than an hour of winding paddles, pushing levers and hauling heavy lock gates, all by hand. But what a brilliant system, lifting and lowering massive boats with nothing but the gentle power of water.

This picturesque stretch feels almost like countryside: three of the original lock keepers' cottages still stand and wildlife thrives here. Looming over it all is the high-walled site of the former County Asylum, England's first pauper lunatic asylum. Signs along the towpath offer historical insights if you need a breather.

CANALS

The route ends at the bottom lock, where the River Brent joins the canal. While the river is non-navigable for powered boats, it can sometimes be explored by paddled craft if water levels allow. Keep an eye out for sudden mudbanks unless you are in the mood for a mud bath. For a more rewarding finale, The Fox pub is a couple of minutes from the water. Cross the bridge over the Brent and head up Green Lane.

Linking routes
- 20 Brentford to Fox Inn at Hanwell (Grand Union/River Brent)
- 21 Hayes to Greenford (Grand Union)

Wildlife highlight
Water conservation
Water has always been a limited resource on the canal network. So vital and precious in fact that, historically, canal companies competed for supply. Originally, canals were built for transporting goods more reliably than natural waterways, with locks, weirs and sluices to control water. But each lock operation uses up water and it goes downhill. Unless the water is pumped back uphill, it is lost out of the canal, so engineers had to get creative. Here at the Hanwell Flight of Locks, for example, they added side ponds to store water temporarily, reducing waste.

ABOVE One of the locks in operation on the flight.

BELOW Paddling next to Three Bridges.

RIGHT Bull's Bridge Junction.

BELOW The Fox Inn pub, Hanwell.

Canal water comes from a mix of reservoirs, rivers and streams, today carefully managed to keep levels navigable and to support wildlife. With climate change bringing warmer summers and unpredictable rainfall, water conservation is even more critical. When water runs low, due to leaks, evaporation or drought, the system is topped up from these sources. Low levels can lead to algal blooms and low oxygen. Occasionally, restrictions are placed on selected sections to save water. Every drop counts.

Tuck in

- **Hayes**: Close to the station, many options on Station Road and Coldharbour Lane.
- **Along the route**, Tesco Extra (Bull's Bridge), The Grand Restaurant And Bar, The Lamb.
- **Hanwell**: Fox Inn.

Paddle provider

- **The Sharks** – thesharks.org.uk

NEED TO KNOW

■ The Canal & River Trust is the navigation authority on the Grand Union Canal. A small craft licence is required, also covered by Paddle UK membership.

■ Follow the navigation rules and keep to the right-hand side in the direction of travel.

■ During the warmer months, a thick carpet of duckweed often covers the canal.

20 BRENTFORD TO FOX INN AT HANWELL GRAND UNION/RIVER BRENT

Fancy a paddle in West London without going on the Thames? Escape the crowds and discover the serene charm of this often overlooked route on the historic Grand Union Canal. Launch from Brentford Basin, paddle the canalised River Brent, stop at The Fox in Hanwell and paddle back. Be prepared for some adventure, with four lock portages. Perfect for those craving a rural feel without venturing far, this quiet and mellow stretch promises a break from the urban hustle all year round.

The Lowdown

DIFFICULTY

WATER TYPE Canalised river

LAUNCH/EXIT Towpath

DISTANCE 7.5km (return)

PORTAGES 2 x 2 (Locks: Clitheroe's, Osterley)

LICENCE REQUIRED? Yes

START/FINISH
- ///names.anyway.casual
- Brentford (National Rail) – 10-min walk via Cornelius Bridge
- Holiday Inn Brentford Lock (underground), Commerce Rd, London TW8 8GA – 5-min walk

A brief history

In the 18th century, goods were transported from the Midlands to London via the Oxford Canal and the River Thames. Delays were common, especially on the section that relied on the tidal Thames. Plans were made to reduce the distance by building a canal. Originally known as the Grand Junction Canal, the shortest canal route between the Thames at Brentford and the industrial city of Birmingham was opened in 1794. Over time, the canal became part of the Grand Union Canal network.

ABOVE Access to River Brent/Grand Union Canal.

to measure the boat's height above the waterline. Today, the toll house at Brentford Lock is one of London's smallest museums, a little piece of canal history.

The paddle

Paddlers Avenue must be the ultimate launch spot for a paddle adventure. You find it at the waterside residential development of Brentford Lock West. Walk down to the canal, set up on the spacious walkway and launch from the floating pontoon located in Brentford Basin, between Paddlers and Boaters Avenues. Head upstream towards the sculpture-like footbridge linking Canal Square and Robin Grove.

The River Brent originates in Hendon and flows to London. It joins the Grand Union Canal at the bottom of the Hanwell Flight of Locks. From there, the River Brent runs its engineered course in parallel with the Grand Union until it meets the Thames at Brentford.

Historically, when passing through Brentford Gauging Lock and toll house, boats were charged a toll on the distance travelled in addition to weight and value of their cargo. To determine the load, the toll keeper used a special gauging rod

The first section is urban with housing and barges lining the basin, new buildings constantly popping up. Mirrored office blocks and a few high-rises compete for limelight as you glide past. Paddle under Bridge No 208A railway bridge and Bridge No 208, which carries the busy Great West Road between London and Bristol.

Boston Manor House is not visible from the canal, but a good slice of their parkland runs along the eastern bank. Ignore the River Brent meandering off to backwaters and portage at Clitheroe's Lock (No 99).

CANALS

OPPOSITE TOP
Getting ready.

OPPOSITE BOTTOM
Brentford Project.

RIGHT
Gallows footbridge.

The west side of the canal is industrial, while greenery dominates the opposite side. You can hear the humming of M4 traffic along this section. Watch out for the weir where the river rejoins the main channel, especially after heavy rain.

The elegant Gallows footbridge, Bridge No 207, offers a glimpse into history. The roving bridge was designed to enable tow horses to cross the canal when the towpath changed sides. Despite the distant clattering of the Piccadilly Line over the elevated structure of Bridge No 206A, an abundance of bird species remains undisturbed. Swans, mallards, moorhens, coots, cormorants and herons are common. It feels like being out in the country.

The canal cuts through a tranquil landscape. Up ahead, every surface of Bridge No 206 with the M4 overhead is decorated with colourful graffiti. The rumbling of traffic heightens, but only fleetingly. The river takes a detour into the backwaters of Osterley Lock Orchard. Stay in the main channel and prepare to portage at Osterley Lock (No 98). This time, it is a bit of a hike on the towpath and Bridge No 205C, Sidebridge Lock.

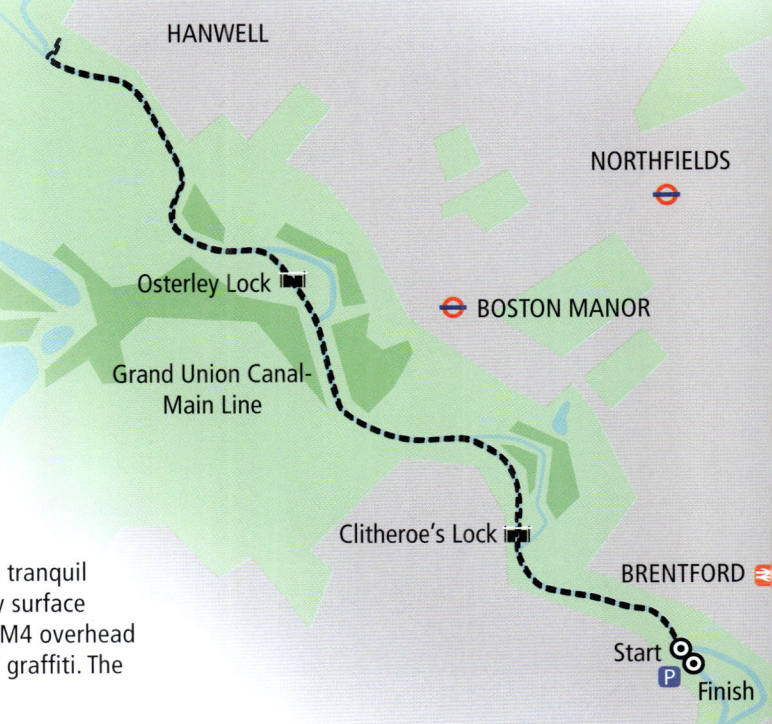

from the canal for good, while the canal starts its slow climb up six locks (see route 19). Exit the water by the lock for a well-deserved break at the charming Fox Inn.

To conclude the adventure, retrace your paddle strokes to Brentford. Once back in Brentford Basin, paddle past the starting point to admire Brentford Gauging Lock and the toll house, one of London's smallest museums. If you want to extend the route, take a quick detour into the Brentford Project on the other side of the lock.

Linking route

- 19 Hayes to Hanwell (Grand Union)

Wildlife highlight

Cormorant (*Phalacrocorax carbo*)
Cormorants are striking black waterbirds that seem to have stepped out of prehistoric times. These coastal-breeding seabirds have found a home in many London waterways. On this route, you often see them perched on the edge of the canal, wings stretched out. This peculiar pose is not just for show, it is their routine for drying feathers. Surprisingly, their plumage is only partially waterproof.

Continue paddling as the canal curves around the nature reserve of Elthorne Waterside before entering a more industrial section. Enjoy the beautiful final stretch with urban meadows and lush greenery. Just before reaching the halfway point at Lock No 97, Hanwell Flight, the River Brent separates

CANALS

Ask any angler, the cormorant is a skilled fisher. With a quick dive into the canal, cormorants swim underwater, easily resurfacing 25m away with a catch in their mouth. These birds are a resident in the area throughout the year.

Tuck in

Pack your own snacks, as there are no places to grab a bite or drink along the paddle until you reach The Fox. This Victorian pub is easily located just steps from the canal on Green Lane in Hanwell. Their all-weather garden is perfect for taking a break with drinks and food. In winter, the garden is covered and heated, giving it a cosy ski chalet vibe.

For before or after paddle fuelling, there are great options at Brentford Lock, Brentford High Street or the new quarters of the Brentford Project.

Paddle providers

- Active360 – active360.co.uk
- London Kayak School – londonkayakschool.com

NEED TO KNOW

- The Canal & River Trust is the navigation authority on the Grand Union Canal. A small craft licence is required, also covered by Paddle UK membership.

- Follow the navigation rules: stay on the right side and give way to boats.

- Portage points are not signposted on this route, so take care to find a safe spot. Lock portage at Osterley Lock involves getting on and off the water with high edges.

OPPOSITE TOP
Turning point at the bottom of Hanwell Flight of Locks.

OPPOSITE BOTTOM
Race a boat.

TOP RIGHT
Street art adds colour to the paddle.

RIGHT
You can't resist posing at Paddlers Avenue.

21 HAYES TO GREENFORD GRAND UNION

Discover a fresh perspective on West London: Hayes, Southall, Northolt and Greenford. This 8.5km one-way route, first on the main branch and then along the Paddington Arm of the Grand Union Canal, offers a great mix of urban and rural scenery. Navigate through the many green pockets and see former industrial areas being transformed to modern canal-side developments. Along the way, get a dose of colourful canal boats, wildlife and blue mind.

The Lowdown

DIFFICULTY

WATER TYPE Canal

LAUNCH/EXIT Towpath

DISTANCE 8.5km (one way)

PORTAGES 0

LICENCE REQUIRED? Yes

START
///spits.crib.payer
- Hayes & Harlington (Elizabeth Line) – 5-min walk
- Hayes & Harlington Station Car Park, Viveash Close, Hayes and Harlington UB3 4BX – 5-min walk

FINISH
///rushed.twin.metals
- Greenford (Central Line, National Rail) – 10-min walk
- Check parking apps

A brief history

The arrival of the Grand Junction Canal in Hayes in 1794 ended its quiet rural existence. The canal drove industrial growth, and factories and warehouses sprang up along the new waterway. When the Paddington Arm of the Grand Union Canal was completed in 1801, it became even easier for cargo to travel between London, the Midlands and the North. Hayes developed into a solid industrial locality in the 20th century, with residential districts added to house the workers.

ABOVE Swan taking off.

CANALS 121

ABOVE Turn left to the Paddington Arm of the Grand Union.

The paddle

The West London town of Hayes is a quick 20-minute journey on the Elizabeth Line from Paddington. Exit Hayes & Harlington station, head down Station Road and cross the bridge before taking the stairs to the towpath. Launch downstream to the left on the main branch of the Grand Union Canal. The waterway is increasingly lined with new residential buildings.

At Bull s Bridge Junction, this time you want to turn left onto the Paddington Arm through the stone arch of Bridge No 21. After a short section of a nondescript industrial area, follow the canal meandering gently through a blend of industrial zones, green spaces and new housing developments. The former gasworks site on the towpath side is being converted into a new residential area. Minet Country Park on the west and, further on, Spikes Bridge Park on the east bank add to the rural feel. It is picturesque: colourful canal boats moored along the water's edge and waterfowl gliding by. You may even see some narrowboats in the traditional Roses and Castles style.

ABOVE A break on the canalside.

BELOW Another bridge over the Grand Union.

Do not be surprised if a coconut bobs up next to you. These are often remnants of religious rituals, released into the water during South Asian ceremonies.

Willowtree Marina marks the halfway point of the route and provides a good rest stop. Once back on the water, the green belt carries on along banks. Enjoy the rural feel of paddling through the wildflower meadows, woodlands and sports grounds of the Willow Tree Open Space and King George's Field.

The section after Engineer's Wharf becomes more urban with warehouses and businesses, except for the nature reserve at Bridge No 17A. The traditional wooden footbridge that connected Greenford and Northolt had to be removed and the modern replacement does not quite have the same charm. The final stretch into Greenford is mainly lined with industrial estates. Exit the water on the towpath side opposite the former Hovis factory, now the upmarket Greenford Quay development. During the summer, they have film screenings and food markets at the canal-side amphitheatre.

CANALS

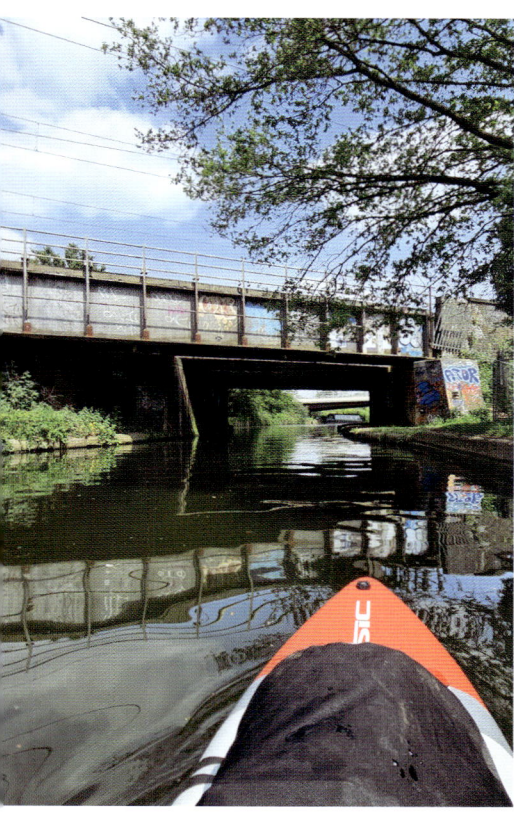

Linking routes
- 19 Hayes to Hanwell (Grand Union)
- 22 Greenford to Harlesden (Grand Union)

Tuck in
- **Hayes**: Close to the station, many options on Station Road and Coldharbour Lane.
- **Along the route**, Tesco Extra (Bull's Bridge), Lock & Quay (Willowtree Marina).
- **Greenford**: Starbucks at Greenford Quay. Close to the station, The Railway Greenford and a few cafés like Caffeine Co.

Paddle provider
- **The Sharks** – thesharks.org.uk

LEFT Solitude on the water.

BELOW Narrowboat moorings.

EED TO KNOW

The Canal & River ⬛st is the navigation ▪thority on the Grand ▪ion Canal. A small ▪ft licence is required, ▪o covered by Paddle ▪ membership.

Follow the navigation ▪es and keep to the ▪ht-hand side in the ▪ection of travel.

During the warmer ▪nths, a thick carpet of ▪ckweed often covers ▪ canal.

22 GREENFORD TO HARLESDEN GRAND UNION

This is a 7km paddle along the mid-stretch of the Paddington Arm of the Grand Union Canal. The route is lock-free and takes you from Greenford through Perivale and Alperton to Harlesden. Experience London suburbia, canal communities, natural beauty and urban charm. It is not all beautiful; paddle past both serene green spaces and gritty industrial sections, capturing the diversity of London. A highlight is crossing the North Circular on an aqueduct.

The Lowdown

DIFFICULTY

WATER TYPE Canal

LAUNCH/EXIT Towpath

DISTANCE 7km (one way)

PORTAGES 0

LICENCE REQUIRED? Yes

START
- ///rushed.twin.metals
- Greenford (Central Line, National Rail) – 10-min walk
- Check parking apps

FINISH
- ///basin.boil.venue
- Harlesden (Bakerloo Line, Lioness) – 6-min walk
- Check parking apps

LEFT Urban scenery on the Paddington Arm.

CANALS

A brief history
In the 18th century, the Grand Junction Canal transformed this rural corner of north-west London. Hay from the green fields was shipped to London to feed the horses, donkeys and mules that towed the canal boats and their manure was returned as fertiliser. Tile and brickworks were common industries.

These days, the canal-side towns along the route are popular London suburbs, surrounded by green spaces and conveniently close to both Central London and Heathrow Airport. New canal-side developments keep emerging.

ABOVE Greenford Quay residential development.

The paddle
From Greenford station, exit on to West Green Place and walk up Greenford Road to find the Grand Union Canal towpath. The launch spot is located by Bridge No 15. Set off east towards Central London.

Some of the urban wilderness along the canal has vanished under bricks and mortar. Greenford Quay, one of the many new canal-side developments, is opposite. There is a waterside amphitheatre with a huge screen.

ABOVE Winter calm: ample room for boards at Grand Junction Arms.

Not a bad spot to watch events or enjoy outdoor cinema during summer evenings.

After Bridge No 16, the scenery transforms from suburbia to hilly parkland. The Horsenden Hill nature conservation site hugs the canal with its wildflower meadows, reed beds and lagoons. You may even see cattle grazing at Horsenden Farm. If paddling here on a weekend, it is hard to resist the local goodies from the farm shop, bakery and brewery.

Carry on east. From the left bank, you might hear the occasional thwack of a ball from Sudbury golf course. Alperton Cemetery is next, mostly hidden from the water's perspective. Residential moorings in various shapes and sizes are a familiar sight, birds claiming abandoned boats. There is a conveniently located supermarket past Bridge No 12.

In Alperton, enjoy street art under Bridge No 11 as you paddle through a stretch lined with high-rises, anonymous warehouses and industrial structures. Cooking aromas linger in the air from food preparation in dark kitchens.

Another shiny new canal-side community follows, aptly named Grand Union. A barge converted into a café in the piazza makes for a pleasant stop.

The canal curves to the right and the iconic Wembley Arch is now behind you. You are approaching the aqueduct that carries the canal over not just the River Brent, but the North Circular. It is a bizarre feeling paddling over one of London's busiest roads.

The final bit is mainly overgrown banks and commercial units. Exit at the Grand Junction Arms before Bridge No 9, because what's a paddle without a well-earned drink to finish? If you don't fancy one, get off the water on the other side.

Linking routes

- 21 Hayes to Greenford (Grand Union)
- 23 Little Venice to Kensal Green (Grand Union)

Wildlife highlight

Eurasian beaver (*Castor fiber*)
Beavers in London? Absolutely. After they were hunted to extinction centuries ago, the Ealing Beaver Project has reintroduced these charismatic creatures to the urban landscape in the Paradise Fields nature reserve. In their new habitat tucked in between the canal and a retail park, beavers are now fulfilling their role as nature's ecological engineers. Usually seen at dawn and dusk, they are busy felling trees, creating canals and building dams, tackling flooding the natural way. Clearly happy with it: in 2024, London welcomed its first baby beavers, or kits, in over four hundred years.

Tuck in

- **Greenford**: Close to the station, The Railway Greenford and a few cafés.
- **Along the route**, street food market at Greenford Quay and Crepes+Coffee at Grand Union.
- **Harlesden**: Grand Junction Arms.

Paddle providers

- **The Sharks** – thesharks.org.uk
- **Ealing Canoe Club** – ealingcanoeclub.org.uk

ABOVE The Ealing Beaver Project.
BELOW Finish at the Grand Junction Arms.

NEED TO KNOW

■ The Canal & River Trust is the navigation authority on the Grand Union Canal. A small craft licence is required, also covered by Paddle UK membership.

■ Follow the navigation rules and keep to the right-hand side in the direction of travel.

■ During the warmer months, a carpet of duckweed often covers the canal.

23 LITTLE VENICE TO KENSAL GREEN GRAND UNION

Tucked away behind the busy Paddington station lies one of Central London's best paddle spots. Completely redeveloped from an abandoned canal terminus, Paddington Basin is now an unexpected contemporary canal-side haven. The 7km return paddle takes you through Little Venice and on to the Paddington Arm of the Grand Union Canal, the green corridor slicing through West London. Never far from the hum of traffic and clatter of skateboards, this route offers a mixture of urban charm, natural calm and unusual public art. While it gets busy with canal traffic around Paddington, there are no portages to tackle. Perfect for a laid-back summer evening.

The Lowdown

DIFFICULTY ●●
WATER TYPE Canal
LAUNCH/EXIT Towpath
DISTANCE 7km (round trip)
PORTAGES 0
LICENCE REQUIRED? Yes
START/FINISH
- ///volume.noises.school
- Paddington (Bakerloo, Central, District, Hammersmith & City Lines, Elizabeth Line, National Rail) – 5–10-min walk; or Warwick Avenue (Bakerloo) – 5-min walk
- Check parking apps

A brief history

Originally, the Grand Junction Canal connected London to Birmingham. Over time, more branches were added, forming the Grand Union Canal. One of these sections, the Paddington Arm, runs 22km from Bull's Bridge Junction in Hayes (see route 21) to Paddington. Completed in 1801, this lock-free cut made it easier for trade to travel between London, the Midlands and the North.

The system was extended further east with the creation of Regent's Canal (see route 24). Browning's Pool in Little Venice joined these two canals and Paddington Basin. Paddington was a major transport hub until the decline of canal trade turned it into a derelict zone with no public access.

Like many disused inland waterways, Paddington Basin has seen extensive redevelopment and is now a modern canal-side hub with Merchant Square and Paddington Central.

CANALS 129

The paddle f arriving at Paddington station, follow signs to the Grand Union Canal. To avoid getting lost in the station maze, take the exit near the Hammersmith & City Line. Once outside, turn left and cross Paddington Central Bridge. Walk along the canal towards Little Venice until you reach the towpath by Rembrandt Gardens, a good place to launch from.

First paddle into Paddington Basin, once the terminus of the Paddington Arm. This lively stretch takes you past Paddington Central to the gleaming high-rises of Merchant Square. It is a bit of a wind tunnel. Expect to see hydraulic footbridges like artwork, people learning to steer electric hire boats and diners watching your paddling skills with admiration. Or

ABOVE Paddington Basin leading to Little Venice.

LEFT High rises of Merchant Square.

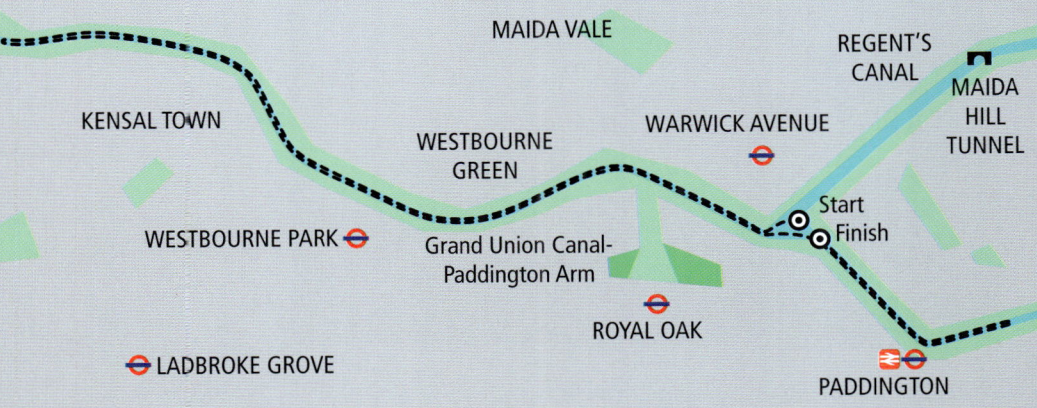

Venice is charming, with narrowboats, a floating puppet theatre and cafés. All set against a backdrop of elegant mansions and weeping willows. Take the first exit west on to the Paddington Arm of the Grand Union Canal under Bridge No 3C. The Canal & River Trust cottage on the left is a former toll station.

You might get curious looks from two popular waterside restaurants, sometimes accompanied with drink-fuelled tips. It is a popular section, an avenue of narrowboats and houseboats lining the canal. There is often an audience on Bridge No 3B, known as Ha'penny Bridge. Continue past the Gothic spire of St Mary Magdalene. The canal bends slightly towards the left by a large housing estate. Stop for a photo opportunity with the heron mural on the residential building between the cable bridge and Bridge No 3.

Paddle past the concrete Westway flyover, the Union Tavern and Meanwhile Gardens beyond Bridge No 4C in Westbourne Park. This green space, transformed from wasteland, has one of London's oldest skate parks. On the right, under the shadow of the brutalist Trellick Tower, is a secret statue garden behind a row of houses. Gerry's

concern. Look out for interesting pieces of public art, like the giant bath plug near Brunel Building, the Alan Turing installation and multiple Paddington Bear statues. That bubble barrier in the water? A system for improving water quality.

On the way back, glide into Browning's Pool in Little Venice and turn left, paddling clockwise around the island. Tour boats have priority, so be courteous. Not quite as grandiose as its Italian namesake, Little

TOP LEFT Avenue of houseboats and canal boats.

LEFT Gerry's Pompeii statue garden.

LEFT Autumn's colours on Regent's Canal.

BOTTOM Trellick Tower.

Pompeii, it is called, and you have a unique opportunity to see it this close. During the Notting Hill Carnival, the beat and crowds reach this far.

Follow the canal past Bridge No 4B and old terraced Victorian houses on Harrow Road. The halfway point of this route is the Sainsbury's supermarket after Bridge No 4. On the opposite side is the Kensal Green Cemetery, rather romantically overgrown. The discarded jetty was where coffins once arrived by water.

Take a break before returning to Rembrandt Gardens. Merchant Square in the summer, with its big screen, deckchairs and bean bags, is perfect for après-paddle relaxation.

Linking route
- 24 Camden to Maida Hill Tunnel (Regent's)

Wildlife highlight

Warm summers
Nothing better than soaking up sunshine in London during the summer, but dry, hot weather plays a surprisingly major role in the health of the Grand Union and London's other canals. As entirely man-made waterways, canals rely on reservoirs to maintain water levels, with the Canal & River Trust monitoring conditions closely. Lack of rainfall can lead to low water, stagnant sections and reduced oxygen levels, affecting fish and other wildlife. Water loss is a constant challenge, as much of the canal network is over two hundred years old and not exactly watertight. In drought conditions, navigation restrictions may be needed to protect the waterways. A warm summer is great for paddling, but the canal needs water, too.

Tuck in

- **Canal-side bars**, restaurants, cafés and street food at Merchant Square in Paddington Basin.
- **Floating restaurants** and a grassy amphitheatre surrounded by places to eat, drink and picnic in Paddington Central.
- **Along the route**, Waterside Café, The Waterway, The Summerhouse, The Union Tavern and Sainsbury's (Ladbroke Grove).

Paddle providers

- **Active360** – active360.co.uk
- **London Sports Trust** – londonsportstrust.org
- **Paddleboarding London** – paddleboardinglondon.co.uk

NEED TO KNOW

■ The Canal & River Trust is the navigation authority on the Grand Union Canal. A small craft licence is required, also covered by Paddle UK membership.

■ Stick to the right-hand side and always give way to powered craft. This busy urban stretch is shared with tour boats, restaurant boats, narrowboats and GoBoats.

■ There is no public access for launching from Paddington Basin. Merchant Square security will quickly let you know if you forget. Head to Rembrandt Gardens instead and mind moored and moving boats when getting on to the water.

■ No swimming, not that many would want to. The canal is just over a metre deep and unexpected items may be lurking below. Wear footwear to avoid surprises.

■ Paddington station is open 24/7. If arriving there, use the exit near the Hammersmith & City Line for the Grand Union Canal. Taking the wrong exit means a very long walk. Once at the canal, cross Paddington Central Bridge to Rembrandt Gardens.

■ Avoid this route during the IWA Canalway Cavalcade in May.

■ Paddled craft are not permitted through Maida Hill Tunnel on Regent's Canal. CRT pre-authorisation is required but rarely granted. Check tunnel signage for details.

ABOVE Return to Merchant Square for a relaxing end to the paddle.

24 CAMDEN TO MAIDA HILL TUNNEL REGENT'S

There is no other paddle location like Camden. The colourful canvas of graffiti and the lively energy of Camden Market create a one-of-a-kind urban setting. An eccentric selection of stalls, shops and restaurants stretches across cobbled yards and old industrial spaces. Here, strolling the streets in a full wetsuit draws no attention. Paddling into leafy Regent's Park and London Zoo provides a peaceful escape. The contrast between the urban buzz and natural calm makes for an epic inner-city paddle. This route packs an incredible amount into just 5.5km.

The Lowdown

DIFFICULTY 💧💧
WATER TYPE Canal
LAUNCH/EXIT Towpath
DISTANCE 5.5km (round trip)
PORTAGES 0
LICENCE REQUIRED? Yes
START/FINISH
📍 ///sits.shaky.blast
🚆 Camden Town (Northern Line) – 10-min walk or Camden Road (Mildmay) – 12-min walk
🅿️ Check parking apps

A brief history

Camden's industrial past is written along the banks of the Regent's Canal. The stretch between Little Venice and Camden was opened in 1816. The canal allowed trade to travel from the Midlands through the Grand Union Canal to the Thames at Limehouse.

Once the canal transport declined, Camden started its transformation into London's most

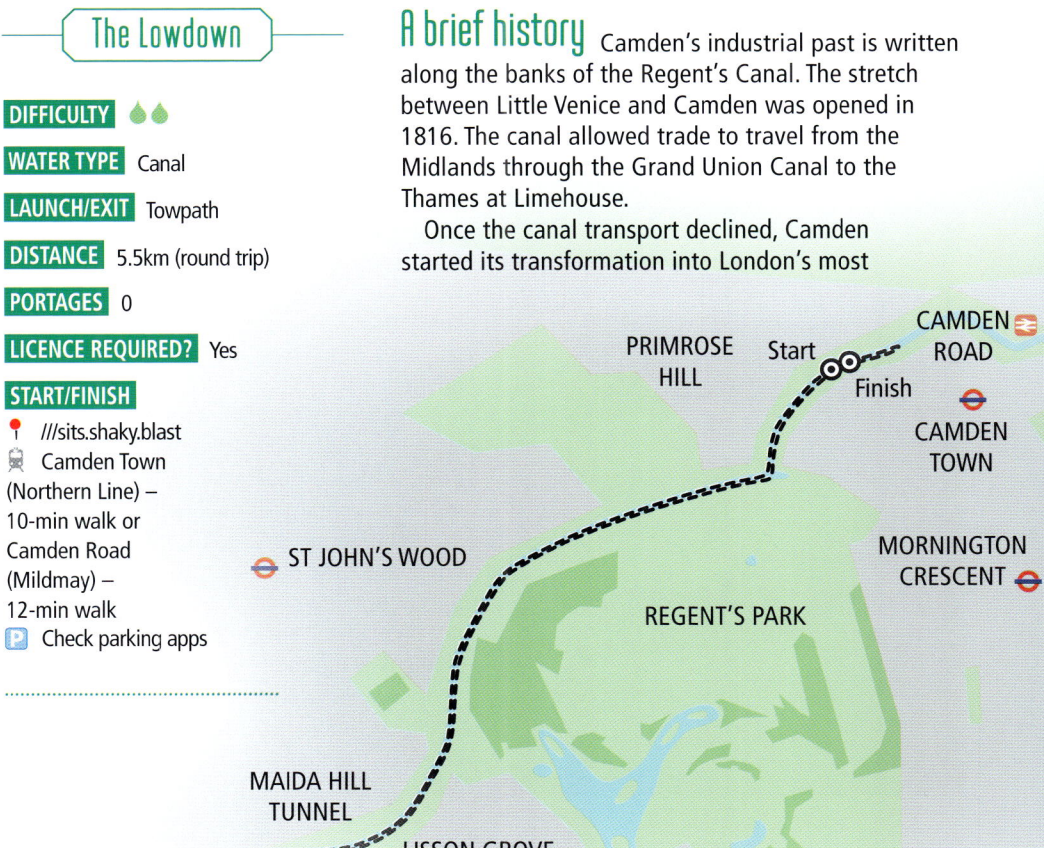

iconic alternative culture centre. From the Roundhouse to venues like the Electric Ballroom and the Underworld, the music scene in Camden is still a defining feature.

Camden Market traces its roots back to the 1970s. From a humble arts and crafts fair, it has blossomed into London's biggest market and fourth most-visited tourist attraction. Despite makeovers, Camden's unpolished charm persists.

The paddle

Alongside the famous lock, Camden Market lines the Regent's Canal. You may see a few remaining punk rockers wearing mohawks and studded jackets posing on the bridge with a sign 'Help a punk get drunk'. Walk along the canal and launch from the north bank towpath opposite the Pirate Castle, a charity for canal activities. It is very busy on the towpaths during weekends, especially in summer.

Head west under Railway Bridge No 18 and paddle through picturesque Primrose Hill. One of the quaintest stretches of the

canal, the south bank is lined with Victorian terraced houses, weeping willows and envy-inducing gardens. When canal traffic has eased on a warm summer's evening, it feels like being in a Claude Monet painting. Spot the life-sized cow statue on one of the balconies?

The towpath side is filled with a changing array of narrowboats, barges and makeshift vessels. In popular areas, free mooring is usually capped at seven days. Boaters without a permanent mooring are called continuous cruisers. These boats are homes, so give them a wave, but respect their privacy.

Continuing upstream, pass under Bridge No 14, known as Prince Albert Bridge, after St Mark's Church and then make a right turn. Mind the canal traffic here. The professionally skippered boats typically announce their arrival with a long horn blast, but many recreational boaters may not give advance notice. There's always an element of unpredictability!

At Cumberland Basin, the pagoda-style floating Chinese restaurant Feng Shang Princess provides a cool backdrop for an urban paddle photo. There is a resident grey

CANALS

heron here, standing motionless, scanning the basin for food. On hot days, you may also catch a terrapin basking in the sun.

Follow the canal through London Zoo. A London landmark since the 1960s, the Grade II listed structure is now Monkey Valley, playground to colobus monkeys. On the other side, the enclosures of wild African dogs and warthogs are visible from the canal perspective. Not exactly the types of animals one would expect to see on a casual paddle in London.

The section of Regent's Park beyond the zoo is the least urban on the canal. The lush greenery of the landscape is so peaceful, it is difficult to believe this is Central London. Keep an eye out for Macclesfield Bridge, nicknamed Blow Up Bridge. Why the name? In October 1874, a barge carrying gunpowder exploded and destroyed the original bridge. It was rebuilt and the incident led to Parliament passing the Explosives Act 1875, regulating the transport of explosives.

OPPOSITE TOP The Pirate Castle in Camden.

LEFT Serenity of Blow Up Bridge.

TOP Feng Shang Princess floating restaurant at Cumberland Basin.

RIGHT Regent's Park's villas and autumn's colours.

The six Regent's Park villas on Outer Circle overlook the canal. Built between 1988 and 2004, they pay homage to John Nash, the 19th-century architect of Regent's Park. Each private residence represents a different classical architectural style. Can you tell Corinthian from Veneto?

The route passes under a series of railway bridges before the final hidden-away section at Lisson Grove. This charming mooring site with houseboats and cute gardens in St John's Wood is one of very few situated on the towpath side. In contrast, behind looms the electrical substation. Ahead is the short Eyre's Tunnel with the Upside-Down House, the only house spanning the Regent's Canal. Traverse with caution for powered craft.

The halfway point of this trip is the mouth of the 249m Maida Hill Tunnel. Check the signage for current rules, but at the time of writing, no unpowered craft was allowed through the tunnel. Turn back and enjoy this epic urban paddle in reverse. Be sure to capture a photo at Roving Bridge in Camden before wrapping up the journey.

Linking routes

- 23 Little Venice to Kensal Green (Grand Union – portage Maida Hill Tunnel)
- 25 Camden to King's Cross (Regent's)

BELOW Spot any colobus monkeys at Monkey Valley?

OPPOSITE Paddling under the railway tracks.

CANALS 137

Wildlife highlight

Black-and-white colobus (*Colobus guereza*) A troop of black-and-white colobus settled into Monkey Valley at ZSL London Zoo in 2022. Observing these long-tailed African creatures this up close from the canal is incredible. It looks like they are flying, leaping smoothly from branch to branch, lounging, socialising and napping in their treetop-inspired habitat. The unique things you experience on a London paddle!

Tuck in

You are never short of options to eat and drink at Camden Market. There are hundreds of restaurants, cafés, rooftop bars and street food stalls. Whatever the latest food craze, it'll be here. You may even discover the next big thing! For calmer ambience, explore the neighbouring Primrose Hill or have a picnic on the hill with the view of the city that never disappoints.

Paddle providers

- **The Pirate Castle** – thepiratecastle.org
- **Paddleboarding London** – paddleboardinglondon.co.uk

NEED TO KNOW

■ The Canal & River Trust is the navigation authority on Regent's Canal. A small craft licence is required, also covered by Paddle UK membership.

■ Follow the navigation rules and keep to the right-hand side in the direction of travel. This busy urban stretch is shared by tour boats, other commercial craft, restaurant boats, narrowboats and GoBoats.

■ Always give way to powered craft. Steered from the back, canal boats often have poor visibility.

■ Swimming is not permitted in the canal. Wear footwear while paddling to avoid unexpected items below the water's surface, in case you take an unintentional dip. Water is just over a metre deep. Bikes, shopping trolleys, cans and glass are sadly common.

■ Paddled craft are not permitted through Maida Hill Tunnel on Regent's Canal. CRT pre-authorisation is required but rarely granted. Check tunnel signage for details.

25 CAMDEN TO KING'S CROSS REGENT'S

This short and sweet urban route celebrates the transformation of Regent's Canal over two centuries. The paddle sets off from a redeveloped part of the famous Camden Market in north-west London. Travelling downstream, King's Cross is the final destination. Once the centre of Victorian trade, then a derelict industrial site, this busy canal-side neighbourhood is now an attractive urban oasis mixing old and new. Traces of its industrial past remain and nature finds surprising footholds among the bricks and mortar. Expect three lock portages along this one-way route.

A brief history

The Regent's Canal is a 14km man-made waterway that runs from Little Venice to Limehouse. A latecomer to the UK canal network, the second stretch between Camden and Limehouse was completed in 1820. This essential trade route carried coal, timber and building materials between the Midlands, London and beyond until the railways took over.

Camden Lock was the original site of a modest crafts and antiques market in the 1970s. It has since expanded into London's largest market, comprising Lock, Stables, Hawley Wharf and Buck Street retail markets. Today, it is the most visited and beloved area on the canal.

King's Cross boasts a rich industrial history, with the construction of the world's largest gasworks in 1824. The gasholders still grace the skyline, reminders of an era when gas was produced and stored here until it was needed to heat and light London.

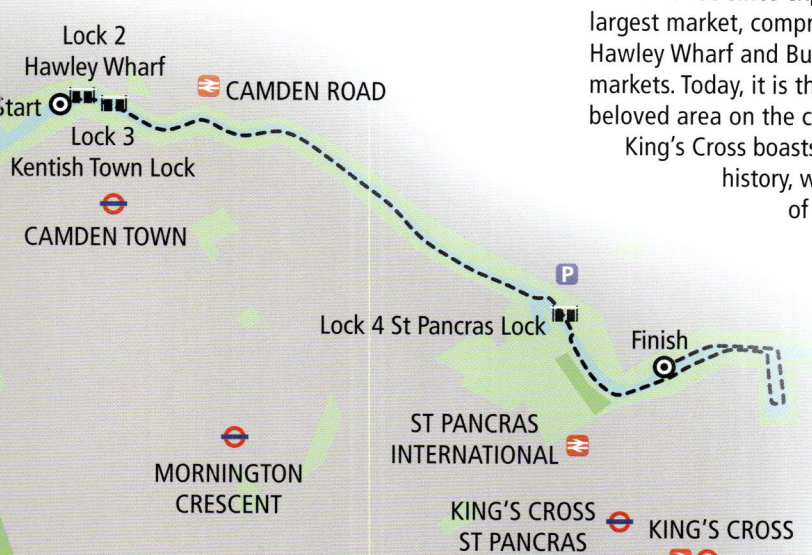

With the addition of a major railway terminus a few years later, King's Cross became a vital hub for transport by canal, rail and road.

The paddle

On Camden High Street, walk past the eccentric shopfronts and continue towards the Camden Lock landmark sign. At the railway bridge, turn east of Chalk Farm Road and onto Water Lane. This newer and more polished slice of Camden Market will lead you through the Hawley Wharf complex on to the quay. The starting point of this paddle route is the canal-side towpath in front of the Waterside Hall East. Opening hours allowing, public toilets are available inside the hall.

Unpowered craft are not permitted to use locks. Since Hawley Lock (No 2) and Kentish Town Lock (No 3) are located so close to one another here, it is better to walk past Bridge No 25 to launch east towards King's Cross. Minding any boats and the weir, get on to the water and across to navigate on the right-hand side of the canal. Get your bearings below the 80s-style high-tech Grand Union Walk housing complex overlooking the water. Although not permitted by the Canal & River Trust, it is typical to see people magnet fishing here. The weird and wonderful items they pull out of the water.

The Lowdown

DIFFICULTY

WATER TYPE Canal

LAUNCH/EXIT Towpath

DISTANCE 2.5km (one way)

PORTAGES 3 (Locks: Hawley, Kentish Town, St Pancras)

LICENCE REQUIRED? Yes

START
- ///wool.fried.vent
- Camden Town (Northern Line) – 5-min walk; Camden Road (Mildmay) – 10-min walk
- Check parking apps

FINISH
- ///noisy.loft.under
- King's Cross St Pancras (Circle, Hammersmith & City, Metropolitan, Northern, Piccadilly & Victoria Lines) – 8-min walk; London King's Cross (National Rail) – 8-min walk; London St Pancras International (National Rail, Eurostar) – 8-min walk
- Handyside Car Park, 3 Canal Reach, London Borough of Camden, London N1C 4BA, height restriction 2.03m – 10-min walk

ABOVE The eclectic Camden High Street.

LEFT In winter wrap up and hit the canal.

OPPOSITE RIGHT Canal-side living along Regent's Canal.

Paddle under Bridge No 27 leading to the Overground station. The atmosphere becomes calmer as the canal winds through residential areas. After the vibrancy and energy of Camden, the long, straight stretch may seem dull, with warehouses and offices dominating the scene. Can you believe that one of the offices is officially called the Ugly Brown Building?

After passing through the tunnel-like Railway Bridge No 32, the scenery changes. Gone is the raw setting when King's Cross was known for warehouse raves and all-night clubbing. The area is undergoing massive regeneration. The gigantic Victorian gasholders have been restored into apartments and, within the largest frame, a park. Gasholder Park is a tranquil green space, perfect for taking a paddle break. Formerly a coal store, the canal-side Coal Drops Yard is a boutique shopping and foodie hotspot. Public toilets are available within the centre.

But first, portage at St Pancras Lock (No 4). While the side with the cute lock keeper's cottage may be tempting, the towpath-side is simpler unless it's crowded with pedestrians and cyclists. Then pass under the beautiful Bridge No 34, Somers Town footbridge, connecting Coal Drops Yard to Camley Street Natural Park. In the 1970s, it was nearly turned into a lorry park but now is a London Wildlife Trust reserve. This urban oasis exists thanks to local campaigners.

Follow the canal as it bends left past the colourful canal boats. The elevated park of Bagley Walk is built on an old railway viaduct. The red pedestrian bridge spanning the canal is like a sculpture, appropriately named Espérance, meaning 'hope' in French, after the Covid lockdowns. During the summer months, you might find an audience at the Granary Square grassy steps, which double as seats for the free 'Screen on the Canal' festival featuring films and sports events. The water is shallow around the edges here. If possible, stick to the centre of the canal to avoid providing unintentional entertainment for the spectators.

The canal widens briefly before narrowing again at Bridge No 36. Guess why it widens? You are paddling on a railway aqueduct – trains to and from King's Cross travel underneath. Battlebridge Basin opens on the right and is a must-visit for those interested in the history of London's inland waterways. It is a narrowboat mooring and home to the Canal Museum in a former ice warehouse. Take a spin in the serene basin before heading back to King's Cross.

On the return journey, paddle past Word on the Water, a floating bookshop, moored on the right-hand side towpath. You can see King's Cross station and St Pancras Renaissance Hotel across the canal. Get off the water in front of The Lighterman at Granary Square. If it's a hot day, the interactive water feature in the square is fun for cooling off. Also, keep an eye out for contemporary art scattered throughout the area for a little culture infusion.

Linking routes
- 24 Camden to Maida Hill Tunnel (Regent's)
- 26 Islington to Hackney (Regent's – portage Islington tunnel)

Wildlife highlight
Floating ecosystems
Did you see the floating reed beds along the canal at Camley Street Natural Park? These artificial wetlands mimic natural ecosystems. They provide shelter for fish, birds and invertebrates. They also help keep the water clean by absorbing extra nutrients. Plus, they bring a green touch to the canal.

Tuck in
You never run out of food and drink options at Camden Market. For a quieter meal, check out the covered food courts at Hawley Wharf. In King's Cross, there are many upmarket restaurants at Coal Drops Yard, but you'll also find Canopy Market and Lower Stable Street Market with options for every budget. And don't forget the lovely outdoor spots where you can enjoy your own food by the canal or squares along the route.

Paddle provider
- **Paddleboarding London** – paddleboardinglondon.co.uk

NEED TO KNOW

■ The Canal & River Trust is the navigation authority on Regent's Canal. A small craft licence is required, also covered by Paddle UK membership.

■ Follow the navigation rules and keep to the right-hand side in the direction of travel. Always give way to powered craft. Steered from the back, canal boats often have poor visibility. A few commercial tour boats operate on this section.

■ The Canal & River Trust does not allow paddled craft to pass through Islington tunnel.

■ During the warmer months, from summer through to autumn, paddling on this route can be challenging due to a thick green carpet of duckweed on the canal. Duckweed multiplies rapidly in the heat. The Canal & River Trust typically does not extend their duckweed-removing service to this section of Regent's Canal.

26 ISLINGTON TO HACKNEY REGENT'S

It is easy to fall in love with this part of London. This charming paddle route explores the eastern section of the Regent's Canal from Islington to Hackney. Lined with old warehouse buildings repurposed into apartments, offices and creative hubs, the canal offers a tranquil corridor to paddle through areas full of character. Stop for food, drinks or ice cream at the many eateries, cafés and bars along the way. There are two lock portages on this urban one-way paddle.

The Lowdown

DIFFICULTY

WATER TYPE Canal

LAUNCH/EXIT Towpath

DISTANCE 2km (one way)

PORTAGES 2 (Locks: City Road, Sturts Lock)

LICENCE REQUIRED? Yes

START
- ///outfit.scenes.clip
- Angel (Northern Line) – 8-min walk.
- Check parking apps

FINISH
- ///lovely.eaten.unfair
- Haggerston (Windrush) – 6-min walk; Old Street (Northern Line, National Rail) – 25-min walk
- Check parking apps

LEFT Classic London canal scenery in Islington.

A brief history

When constructing the second stretch of the Regent's Canal from Camden to Limehouse in the 1810s, engineers faced a challenge at Islington Hill – how to get the canal to the other side? They considered three options: a long detour around, a series of locks over or a tunnel under. The tunnel won, and in 1820 the 878m Islington Tunnel opened beneath what is now Angel in Islington.

With no towpath in the tunnel, horses had to be led over the hill while boat crews resorted to 'legging it' – lying on planks and pushing the boat through with their legs. The phrase lives on, though the method was later replaced by a steam chain tug for a safer and more efficient passage.

The New River, built in 1613 to bring fresh water from Hertfordshire (see route 30) to North London, has its head beneath what is now Sadler's Wells in Islington.

The paddle

The start point of this paddle is the towpath where the canal resurfaces at the eastern portal of Islington Tunnel. Head down the slope to the canal from Colebrooke Row Gardens in Angel. Staying well clear of the mouth of the tunnel and any boats entering or exiting, launch downstream towards Bridge No 38. Navigate along Vincent Terrace Woods on the south. For a borough with the least green space per capita in the country, this Islington paddle offers a surprisingly lush experience.

ABOVE City Road Basin in Islington.

The first portage approaches quickly at City Road Lock (No 5). Surrounded by weeping willows, the lock is a popular hangout place for locals. There is a real buzz with barges serving food and drink, tables and chairs scattered on the towpath. Pause for a chat with the Canal & River Trust volunteers, who are always eager to swap stories. After passing the lock-side café, find a safe spot to relaunch on to the water.

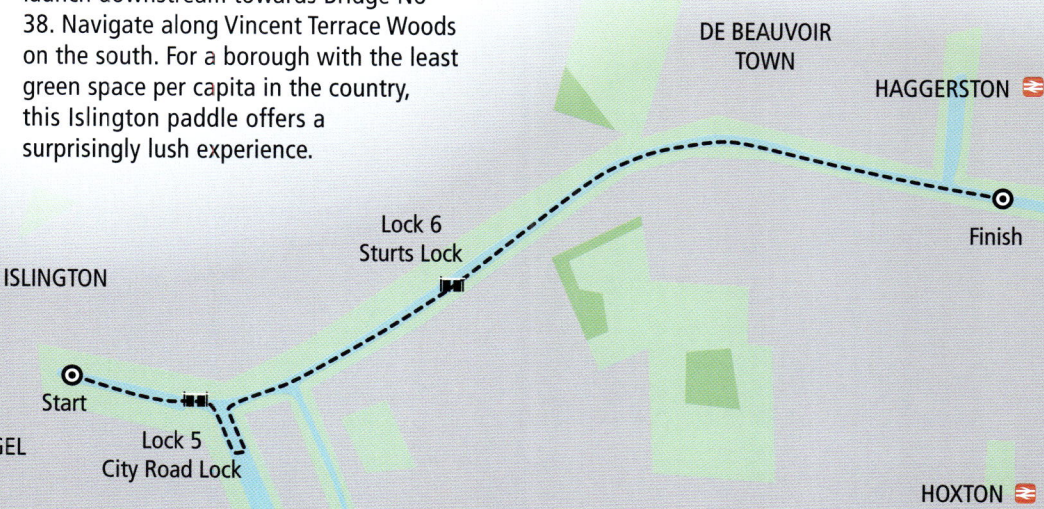

City Road Basin on the south side marks the halfway point on the canal's journey from Little Venice to Limehouse. You are likely to encounter other paddlers, as Islington Boat Club runs sessions here. Specialising in community paddles, you can join SUP at Islington all year round or come for a litter pick on the water. Nothing better than SUP with a side of sustainability. The basin gets particularly lively and festive on the first Sunday in September during the annual Angel Canal Festival. Separated by Wharf Road, the next basin is Wenlock Basin, such a picturesque urban setting with narrowboat moorings. Can you spot The Shard or other London high-rise landmarks in the distance?

Passing under Bridge No 39, tucked away from the hustle and bustle of London life, is the Narrowboat pub. The section that follows before Sturts Lock is straight, lined with once derelict warehouses now being replaced by residential buildings and offices. Change is constant. There is a unique charm with a bohemian vibe that attracts the creative industries, such as Holborn Studios. If you paddle here in the evening, moor up and treat yourself to a break in their quayside restaurant and pontoon bar.

The portage at Sturts Lock (No 6), is again on the north towpath side. It's fascinating to watch a narrowboat navigate a lock, such an impressive operation. Gone are the days of resident lock keepers in their quaint cottages. Nowadays, volunteer teams may occasionally assist at the busiest spots of the canal. First come, first served? Not at locks. The goal is to save water. If the lock is empty, the boat travelling upstream gets it first. If it is already full, the boat heading downstream gets right of way. Lock sharing is encouraged.

The unassuming apartment building with the gym on the ground floor after the lock is Gainsborough Studios. If you are into classic suspense films, you may want to get off the water and take a photo of the massive Alfred Hitchcock sculpture tucked away in the courtyard. This location used to be known locally as Los Islington, back when it was a famous film studio.

Follow the canal downstream, with De Beauvoir Town situated on the north and Hoxton on the south side. The scenery maintains its urban vibe. Modern residential buildings coexist with a string of brightly painted narrowboats and graffiti-covered sections. After Bridge No 43, the area gets more vibrant. Kingsland Towpath and Kingsland Basin are flanked with waterside restaurants, cafés and pop-ups. On warm summer weekends and evenings, you often meet a curious audience here. Now is not the time to take an accidental dip.

This paddle route concludes in Haggerston. Exit the water on to the towpath once you have cleared Bridge No 45, which carries Kingsland Road. If you want to mark the end of your East London urban adventure, this neighbourhood hosts several bars and taprooms under the London Overground arches.

ABOVE Approaching The Narrowboat pub.

ABOVE You always find patches of nature in urban paddling.

Linking routes

- 25 Camden to King's Cross (Regent's – portage Islington tunnel)
- 27 Hackney to Mile End (Regent's)

Wildlife highlight

Mandarin duck (*Aix galericulata*)
Introduced from China, the mandarin duck escaped or was released from captivity in Britain and is now thriving on waterways like Regent's Canal. It is a magnificent-looking species, especially the male with its handsome crest and vibrant plumage. The female looks a bit duller. Oddly for a duck, it nests in trees and really likes the canal stretches with overhanging trees as hiding spots. Keep a good lookout for this distinctive but shy duck around the water's edge. The mandarin duck can be seen throughout the year.

Tuck in

The food scene is always changing, with plenty of canal-side cafés, restaurants and food barges along the route. Near the launch spot, Upper Street in Islington is a foodie's dream. Haggerston also has great options, especially around the revamped Overground arches. For a top-notch cheese toastie, head to Towpath Cafe.

Paddle providers

- **Islington Boat Club (IBC)** – islingtonboatclub.com
- **SUP at Islington** – islingtonboatclub.com
- **Paddleboarding London at IBC** – paddleboardinglondon.co.uk

NEED TO KNOW

■ The Canal & River Trust is the navigation authority on Regent's Canal. A small craft licence is required, also covered by Paddle UK membership.

■ Follow the navigation rules: stay on the right side and give way to boats. Canal boats, steered from the back, have limited visibility. Some tour boats operate here.

■ No paddling is permitted through the one-way Islington Tunnel.

27 HACKNEY TO MILE END REGENT'S

This is an epic urban paddle from Hackney to Mile End on Regent's Canal. The quirky charm, creative vibe and bohemian atmosphere of these neighbourhoods make the route uniquely East London. The course cuts through some classic urban canal scenes with the iconic Bethnal Green gasholders, colourful graffiti and tranquil green spaces. Victoria Park and Mile End Park line the route, providing a welcome escape from the hectic London pace. The adventure becomes authentically East London with a break at Broadway Market.

The Lowdown

DIFFICULTY

WATER TYPE Canal

LAUNCH/EXIT Towpath

DISTANCE 3.5km (one way)

PORTAGES 2 (Locks: Acton's, Old Ford)

LICENCE REQUIRED? Yes

START
- ///lovely.eaten.unfair
- Haggerston (Windrush) – 6-min walk; Old Street (Northern Line, National Rail) – 25-min walk
- Check parking apps

FINISH
- ///fund.boot.atoms
- Mile End (Central, District, Hammersmith & City Lines) – 8-min walk
- Lawton Road Car Park, 381 Mile End Rd, London E3 4QS, height restriction – 2.10m – 5-min walk

ABOVE Always new masterpieces.

ABOVE There are several entry and exit points along the Regent's Canal towpath.

A brief history
At the height of the industrial era, the canal was completely off-limits to the public as horse-drawn boats transported goods to and from the Midlands. Commercial traffic on Regent's Canal eventually came to an end by the late 1960s when the railways and roads took over. Since then, the once grimy canal-side areas are being redeveloped into waterside homes and businesses. Towpaths are busy with walkers, cyclists and, recently, magnet fishers. And the waterway itself is accessible for leisure, recreation and, of course, canal boat living.

The paddle
This paddle starts on the north bank of the Regent's Canal towpath along Dunston Road in Hackney. If arriving from Haggerston Overground, walk down Stean Street until you reach the canal. Look for the ramp leading to the towpath. Set up and launch downstream past the Laburnum Boat Club towards Limehouse.

Creative expression flourishes along the route. The canal-side structures are like a giant canvas, sprayed with colourful art and provocative slogans. There is always something new to see — be it outdoor art or curiosities. Don't let the life-size sharks at Hoxton Docks after the tunnel-like Bridge No 47 startle you. These sculptures have been at the centre of a long-standing dispute between Antepavilion and Hackney Council – are they art or architecture?

The section before Acton's Lock (No 7) cuts through a mainly residential area. The channel is snug due to narrowboats on both sides. In London, permanent moorings are difficult to come by, so many boaters lead a nomadic lifestyle. Have you seen the bright-orange lifeboat cruising the canals yet?

Before returning to the water after portaging the lock, take a pit stop. Broadway Market, the street running north from the

ABOVE The Bethnal Green gasholders No 2 (1866) and No 5 (1889).

canal to London Fields, has great local small businesses and hosts a well-known weekend market. It is a lovely spot to indulge in a coffee and pastry among the Hackney crowd.

The canal bends southwards. Worth a photo, it is a classic urban canal setting with the iconic Bethnal Green gasholders, their reflection in the water. Next to the gasometers, Containerville is built using upcycled shipping containers. So East London!

Follow the canal under the graffiti-clad Bridge No 50 railway bridges and narrow Bridge No 51. Pound Path, which runs alongside, is popular with cyclists, walkers and families. In boating terminology, a lock-free section like this is called a 'pound'.

Soon, a green oasis borders the east bank. This is Victoria Park, the largest park in Tower Hamlets. The lush, serene scenery stands in stark contrast to the urban environment most expect. On the opposite side, spot all the weird and wonderful things in the waterside gardens. You also have a unique perspective to observe the overgrown plants, graceful weeping willows and the occasional moorhen hiding along the water's edge.

Keep paddling until you arrive at the rural backdrop of Old Ford Lock (No 8). Confusingly, there is another Old Ford Lock (No 19) on the Lee Navigation less than 3km away. Be careful after portaging the lock, because suddenly on the left is the entrance to the Hertford Union Canal (route 29). It is a tight turn for narrowboats taking the shortcut to the Lee Navigation.

On the final section, Mile End Park runs like a green ribbon along the east bank. The Mile End Ecology Park is worth a visit another time. Make sure you spot a sculpture of one of the heroes of the canal age – horses that towed narrowboats laden with cargo. Proper horsepower! The sculpture is part of the nationwide Portrait Bench campaign. Lock No 9, Mile End Lock, is the end point of the paddle. Get off the water before reaching the lock. If departing from Mile End station, walk under the unusual yellow footbridge, officially called the Green Bridge. It is actually covered in plants.

Another East London paddle adventure in the bag.

CANALS

Linking routes
- 26 Islington to Hackney (Regent's)
- 29 Limehouse Loop (Lee Navigation)

Wildlife highlight
Horses
Aside from the sculpture in Mile End Park, the only horses you are likely to see along this route belong to the Met's Mounted Branch. But horses were once the engines of the canal age. Horses, mules and donkeys towed narrowboats carrying 20 tons of cargo, long before motors took over. Smaller animals were preferred for their efficiency – they needed less feed to get the job done. Powered by hay, too. The system relied on water reducing friction, allowing a steady pace to keep boats moving. But it was not without risks; horses sometimes slipped into the canal. Special ramps were built to help them climb back out. Spot these along the banks on your next paddle.

Tuck in
This East London route is packed with places to refuel, from floating cafés to canal-side spots. On weekends, Broadway Market and Victoria Park Market (Sunday) add even more options. Local favourites include Yeast Bakery, Café Cecilia near Broadway Market and the Palm Tree pub in Mile End for a classic Cockney experience.

NEED TO KNOW

■ The Canal & River Trust is the navigation authority on Regent's Canal. A small craft licence is required, also covered by Paddle UK membership.

■ Follow the navigation rules: stay on the right side and give way to boats. Canal boats, steered from the back, have limited visibility.

■ During the warmer months, duckweed often takes over and makes paddling a tough shift along this Regent's Canal section.

Paddle providers
- **Laburnum Boat Club** – laburnumboatclub.com
- **Paddleboarding London** – paddleboardinglondon.co.uk

BELOW A peaceful stretch near Victoria Park.

28 LONDON LEGACY LOOP LIMEHOUSE BASIN

Ready for the London Legacy Loop Challenge, a 10km urban route in East London? This official Paddle UK challenge lets you explore five London waterways in one go, with an online leader board to track your progress. Start the journey at the serene Limehouse Basin, then paddle along London's oldest canal, the Limehouse Cut. Experience the industrial charm mixed with colourful street art, urban redevelopment and rich history along the way. Finish by looping around London Stadium and Queen Elizabeth Olympic Park. The best news? This route is completely portage-free.

A brief history

In the 18th century, barges carrying freight from Hertfordshire to London on the River Lea faced the challenge of relying on tides to reach the River Thames. The final 12km tidal stretch that caused most delays involved navigating the meandering twists and turns of Bow Creek and making a full loop around the Isle of Dogs. In boaters' terms, a 'cut' means a canal because canals were cut out of the land. Limehouse Cut

CANALS 151

The Lowdown

DIFFICULTY 💧

WATER TYPE Canal

LAUNCH/EXIT Towpath

DISTANCE 10km (return)

PORTAGES 0

LICENCE REQUIRED? Yes

START/FINISH
- ///shark.riots.needed
- Limehouse (DLR, National Rail) – 10-min walk
- Check parking apps

The paddle This route starts at the tranquil marina of Limehouse Basin. While not quite Saint-Tropez, you may spot the occasional luxury cruiser or tall ship. The basin is also the gateway to Regent's Canal (see route 29), so make sure to follow the signs to Limehouse Cut. Launch on to the water and pass under Bridge No 9 to enter the first section of the London Legacy Loop. The Limehouse Cut curves northwards at Ropemakers Field before adjusting to its usual straight urban course towards Bromley by Bow.

was in essence constructed as a shortcut from Bow Locks to the site of Limehouse Basin. The canal took 16 months to dig and provided a 2km non-tidal link to the Thames. Completed in 1770, Limehouse Cut is the oldest canal in London.

The maze of waterways that feeds on to the Lee Navigation and the Thames in East London is collectively known as the Bow Back Rivers. The evocative names of these forgotten channels hint at their roles in powering Britain's economy: City Mill River, Pudding Mill River, Three Mills Wall, Prescott Channel, Bow Creek, Channelsea River and Waterworks River. When the industrial landscape shifted, these waterways were left neglected and the area abandoned as industrial wasteland.

The development of Queen Elizabeth Olympic Park for the 2012 London Olympic and Paralympic Games put the Bow Back Rivers back in focus. Tightly integrated into the Olympic Park's layout, these existing waterways were cleaned, repaired and restored.

LEFT Limehouse Cut, bundled up for a winter paddle.

TOP Gliding under one of the many bridges of the route.

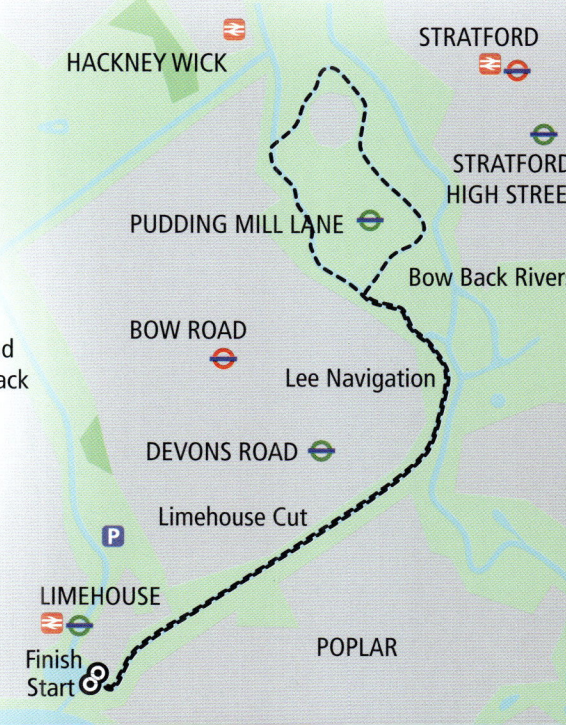

The rhythmic sound of the paddle hitting the water may be accompanied by the vibration of a DLR train crossing Bridge No 7. Along the canal's edge, the old industrial warehouses are alive with gigantic murals and colourful street art. Some have been torn down to make way for new developments, others renovated as modern housing. Luckily, the foul-smelling industries that gave Bridge No 4 the nickname Stinkhouse Bridge are no longer there. Despite canal boats on both sides, the unusual width of the canal creates a feeling of spaciousness. It is very pleasant to paddle.

After you have cleared Bridge No 1 carrying the A12, you have officially left the Limehouse Cut and entered the Lee Navigation. Soon, the white footbridge of Bow Locks is on your right. Do not access Bow Locks. These locks connect the Lee Navigation to the tidal Bow Creek, ebbing and flowing to the Thames. Instead, carry on along the canal. This area is seeing major redevelopment and new buildings are popping up all the time. The dramatic silhouette of a group of seven gasholders are awaiting their fate. They have actually been named among the top ten endangered buildings of the Victorian and Edwardian eras.

The next section is a wonderful jumble of bohemian canal charm, urban regeneration and spots of greenery. The brick building on Three Mills Island is the world's largest surviving tidal mill. There is also a former distillery, now home to a film studio, easily recognisable to any MasterChef fans. Surrounded by the web of Bow Back Rivers, this patch of cobbled streets and Three Mills Green is a lovely spot for a break. The Line sculpture trail features a few pieces here too. On the opposite side on the left is a supermarket if you need to top up the snack supplies and use the facilities.

Follow the canal through Bridge No 5, Bow Flyover. Paddle past the junction of St Thomas Creek, one of the Bow Back Rivers, and continue straight ahead. Another few railway bridges later, you arrive in front of Old Ford Lock. Do not portage here, but turn right on to the Old River Lea. You are soon in Queen Elizabeth Olympic Park, taking a clockwise spin around the iconic London Stadium. Stopping or mooring is prohibited but it is an incredible experience to paddle at the site of the 2012 Olympics.

Admire the double radial guillotine gates of the refurbished Carpenters Road Lock. Leave it on the left and paddle the curve of the canal. You are now navigating on City Mill River, another one of the Bow Back Rivers. You cannot miss the impressive structure of ArcelorMittal Orbit, the tallest sculpture in the UK and home to the world's longest tunnel slide. Behind it looms the London Aquatics Centre.

Soon after passing the railway bridge, turn right at the junction of City Mill Lock.

CANALS 153

RIGHT The historic Three Mills

OPPOSITE The ArcelorMittall Orbit at the Queen Elizabeth Olympic Park.

St Thomas Creek is the final stretch to complete the loop. It takes you back to the meeting point with the Limehouse Cut by Bridge No 5. From here, retrace your way back to Limehouse Basin.

Linking routes
- 27 Hackney to Mile End (Regent's)
- 29 Limehouse Loop (Lee Navigation)

Tuck in
- Food stops are few along the route, but in warmer months, barges near Three Mills Island may serve drinks and snacks. Three Mills Green makes a great picnic spot, with Tesco nearby for supplies. The e5 Poplar Bakehouse is a top choice for coffee, pastries and Canary Wharf views.
- After the Legacy Loop, celebrate at The Grapes on Narrow Street, where the Thames-side terrace offers a glimpse of an Antony Gormley sculpture.

Paddle provider
- **Moo Canoes** – moocanoes.com

NEED TO KNOW

■ The Canal & River Trust is the navigation authority on Limehouse Cut. A small craft licence is required, also covered by Paddle UK membership.

■ Follow the navigation rules: stay on the right side and give way to boats. Canal boats, steered from the back, have limited visibility.

■ During the warmer months, a thick carpet of duckweed often covers the canal, especially on the sections of the Lee Navigation and around Queen Elizabeth Park.

■ At Limehouse Basin Marina, it is usually tranquil, but be cautious when boats are moving, especially during tidal lock operation. Boat access is restricted to four hours either side of high water.

■ The London Legacy Loop is an official Paddle UK challenge. If you want to participate and get on the leader board, register and upload your time on the Go Paddling website.

29 LIMEHOUSE LOOP LEE NAVIGATION

Limehouse Loop, also known as the East London Ring, is a must-paddle for any serious urban explorer. This rare circular route offers a unique perspective of London's urban landscape from five waterways – the Hackney Cut, Lee Navigation, Limehouse Cut, Regent's Canal and Hertford Union Canal. Think street art, historic landmarks, diverse urban scenes and East London vibes. This 10km route includes eight lock portages, but the experience is totally worth it! Public transport advised.

A brief history
The five seemingly random waterways on this route are intertwined in industrial history. Each one was built to make the transport of goods as efficient and cost-effective as possible, supporting London's economic growth.

The Lowdown

DIFFICULTY
WATER TYPE Canal
LAUNCH/EXIT Towpath
DISTANCE 10 km (round trip)
PORTAGES 8 (Locks: Old Ford, Commercial, Salmon Lane, Johnson's, Mile End, Top, Middle, Bottom)
LICENCE REQUIRED? Yes
START/FINISH
- ///just.normal.pound (1)
- ///nest.vision.ports (2)
- Hackney Wick (1) (Mildmay) – 5-min walk; Stratford (Central, Jubilee and Elizabeth Lines, DLR, Mildmay) – 20-min walk
- St Marks Gate Car Park (2), 2 Wick Lane, London Borough of Tower Hamlets London E3 2NB – 5-min walk

It all started with the River Lea, which was canalised under an Act of 1767. The engineered waterway is known as the Lee Navigation, running from Hertford to the River Thames in East London. The canal rapidly became a lifeline for milling, brewing and the transport of commodities like coal, building materials and even gunpowder. The 3km stretch from Lea Bridge to Old Ford Locks is known as the Hackney Cut.

In 1770, the construction of the Limehouse Cut reduced the cargo travel times further, providing a shortcut for boats on the final leg of the Lee Navigation. The new canal took them directly from Bow Locks to the Thames at Limehouse, bypassing the tricky tidal currents of Bow Creek.

Fast-forward to 1820 and London welcomed yet another canal: Regent's Canal. This waterway, stretching from Little Venice to Limehouse, opened up trade routes all the way from the Midlands via the Grand Union Canal to the Thames.

The final piece of London's canal network was the Hertford Union Canal, also known as Duckett's, added in 1830, linking the eastern section of Regent's Canal to the Lee Navigation.

The paddle

The launch point of this paddle is Hackney Wick. Known for its wharves and warehouses in the industrial era, the Wick today scores high on urban credentials. The canal-side is buzzing with hip eateries, terraces, food trucks and barges. Head towards The Milk Float and Barge East to find a safe, vacant spot to take off from. There are nice grassy areas to set up on, with the London Stadium as a backdrop.

Taking a clockwise approach to the route, start your journey south on the Hackney Cut on the Lee Navigation. You want to be travelling towards Limehouse Basin, between the Olympic Park on the left and Fish Island on the right.

ABOVE By Barge East, a patch of greenery to set up on.

Fish Island is no typical island getaway. In fact, it is not even an island. Transformed from sooty industrial roots to one of the largest creative clusters in the country, it is now filled with sleek new developments. Amid the rapid regeneration, the street-art-covered warehouses after Bridge No 10 are full of original character.

Approaching Old Ford Lock (No 19), remember the 1990s 'Big Breakfast' TV show? It used to be broadcast from the lock

ABOVE Gliding through Hackney Wick's industrial past.

house. Portage here, cross the bridge, ignore the exit to the Olympic Park and continue straight down. The green area on the left is the Old Ford Island nature reserve.

Enjoy the gently meandering section, paddle under railway bridges No 8 and 7 and past the junction of St Thomas Creek on your left. Stay on the Lee Navigation through Bridge No 5, Bow Flyover. The landscape is in a constant state of flux, construction projects shaping the landscape. The historic Three Mills Island still stands proud, testament to the canal's heritage within the maze of Bow Back Rivers. The east bank park area close to the Waterbus stop is ideal for a break. There is also a supermarket on the right-hand side where you can pick up supplies and use the facilities.

The group of gasholders towering in the east is such a classic urban canal scene. Stay on the right as you glide past the white footbridge of Bow Lock and the locks themselves. Avoid the tidal Bow Creek and instead carry on straight. At Bridge No 1, you are officially joining the Limehouse Cut. London's oldest canal, it is 2km long and lock-free. Soak in the urban sights in the shadow of Canary Wharf and relish the portage-free ride while it lasts.

One final bend at the end of the Cut leads you to Limehouse Basin, the halfway point of the trip. It is also the hub of three London waters – Limehouse Cut, the Thames (no access for paddlers) and Regent's Canal. Once you have cruised around admiring the vessels moored in the marina, follow the signposting to Regent's Canal.

The fourth section of the route takes you north towards Victoria Park. The upcoming portage-fest starts with two lock portages in quick succession. The excitement kicks off with Commercial Lock (No 12), followed by Salmon Lane Lock (No 11), some 200m later. The scenery is residential. Things take a greener turn around Johnson's Lock (No 10), where Mile End Park lines the eastern bank. Before tackling the final portage on Regent's Canal at Mile End Lock (No 9), treat yourself to a break at the shaded picnic area on the towpath side, just past Bridge No 57.

Don't miss the entrance to Hertford Union Canal on the right. The final waterway is a humble canal at just 2km long but packed with character. It runs alongside leafy Victoria Park. With the houses and gardens hugging the water's edge, you are peering into a slice of local life. Portage at the aptly named

LEFT Portaging at Old Ford Lock.

OPPOSITE Regent's Canal, tranquillity in the heart of the city.

CANALS

Top (No 1), Middle (No 2) and Bottom (No 3) Locks. The stretches between them are a changing canvas of colourful graffiti art.

Arrive at the junction of Hackney Cut and exit the water back in Hackney Wick.

Linking routes
- 27 Hackney to Mile End (Regent's)
- 28 London Legacy Loop (Limehouse Basin)

Wildlife highlight
Canada goose (*Branta canadensis*)
Originally from North America, Canada geese are a familiar sight on London's waterways year-round. Despite being waterfowl, they actually spend half their time on terra firma. Unsurprisingly, not everyone is a fan. A group of geese is called a gaggle and they tend to gather in large, noisy flocks, leaving quite a mess behind.

Canada geese are known for monogamy, often mating for a decade or more. Come spring, females lay up to 10 eggs and incubate them for almost a month without leaving the nest. During this time, males can get protective, especially around paddlers. Goslings stick with their parents for a year, then join other juvenile geese until they are ready to settle down.

Tuck in
- There is no shortage of canal-side bars and eateries in the trendy Hackney Wick. If you want to moor up with your craft for an after-paddle treat, some popular venues include The Milk Float, with a heated roof terrace, and CRATE Brewery, with stone-baked pizzas and craft beers. For pub-style food and drink, the Lord Napier pub is hard to miss. The building is covered entirely in street art, inside and out.

NEED TO KNOW

■ The Canal & River Trust is the navigation authority for the waterways on this route. A small craft licence is required, also covered by Paddle UK membership.

■ Follow the navigation rules: stay on the right side and give way to boats. Canal boats, steered from the back, have limited visibility.

■ During the warmer months, a thick carpet of duckweed often covers the canals, making paddling impossible. Spring, early summer, late autumn and winter are better times to paddle here.

■ Check the London Stadium events schedule for timings to avoid crowds on public transport.

- On the route, don't miss e5 Poplar Bakehouse and Ragged Café at the Ragged School Museum.

Paddle provider
- **Moo Canoes** – moocanoes.com

30 HERTFORD TO BROXBOURNE LEE NAVIGATION

Join the Lee Navigation at Hertford as it starts its journey to London. This rural one-way paddle cuts through the villages of Ware and Stanstead Abbotts to reach Broxbourne. The man-made navigation is a wildlife corridor with a diverse landscape. Lined with water meadows, the route features Hertfordshire's history, nature and present. Are you ready for some serious portaging? There are seven locks along the route. In high season, the waters on the lower section may get busy with boaters.

The Lowdown

DIFFICULTY

WATER TYPE Canal/canalised river

LAUNCH/EXIT Towpath

DISTANCE 14km (one way)

PORTAGES 7 (Locks: Hertford, Ware, Hardmead, Stanstead, Feildes Weir, Dobbs Weir, Carthagena)

LICENCE REQUIRED? Yes

START
- ///magic.tops.stud
- Hertford East (National Rail) – 5-min walk
- Hartham Lane Car Park, 2 Hartham Ln, Hertford SG14 1QR – 10-min walk

FINISH
- ///pump.pounds.marble
- Broxbourne (National Rail) – 10-min walk
- Old Mill & Meadows Car Park, Mill Lane, Broxbourne, EN10 7AE – 5-min walk

A brief history

The River Lea originates in the chalk hills of the Chilterns and flows south-east to meet the River Thames in London. Historically, flour from Hertfordshire mills was ferried to London, mainly for beer- and bread-making. The Lea was the first river in the UK to be modified for commercial use. The original Act of Parliament was passed back in 1425 and several navigation improvements followed over the centuries. The artificial channel is called the Lee Navigation. It stretches 44km from Hertford to London's East End, with 20 locks along its course.

In the early 17th century, a solution was needed to supply water to the rising population of London. The New River aqueduct was built to transport fresh water from Hertfordshire springs to Islington solely by the force of gravity. Remarkably, parts of the New River continue to be part of London's water supply infrastructure to this day.

CANALS

The paddle

ABOVE Hertford East Station.

Still within TfL's contactless zone, this route sets off from the historic market town of Hertford, where the Lee Navigation starts its passage to London. The launch spot is down Mill Road, a short walk from Hertford East train station. The area is residential and the shaded towpath is popular among pedestrians and cyclists. The narrow strip of water here is lined with houseboats, so pick a safe and convenient place on the south bank for setting up for the paddle. Pack your board keeping in mind the seven locks along the route. You will be a portage pro after this one!

Heading east, after Hertford Lock (No 1), you'll leave the industrial outskirts of town behind and enter a rural landscape. The navigation cuts through the wide-open spaces of Hartham Common and King's Meads Nature Reserve. Sometimes there are cows grazing on the waterside meadows. Where the route takes a sharp south-east, you might spot a sign inviting you to explore a naturist spot. Newcomers are warmly welcome.

Paddle past a small brick building on the

ABOVE A glimpse of history at the lock keeper's cottage.

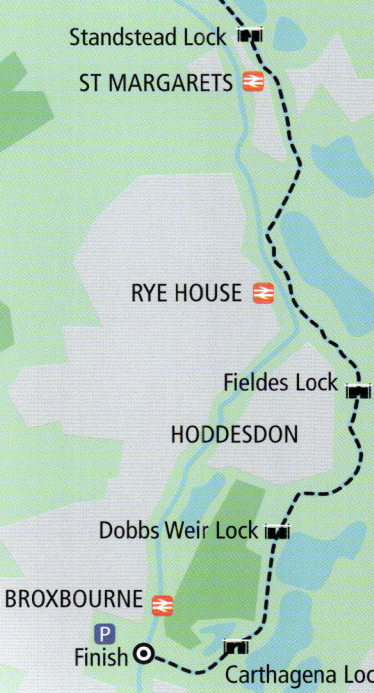

south bank. New Gauge House controls the water flow from the Lee Navigation to the New River, keeping it within statutory limits. Isn't it surprising that the New River (see route 39) still supplies London with some 8 per cent of the capital's fresh water?

After portaging at Ware Lock (No 2), follow the navigation to the leafy town of Ware. Look out for the 18th-century waterside gazebos, once summer houses for the rich. The town comes alive during the warmer months, especially when the Ware Festival rolls around in July.

Nature reserves sit in a mosaic of wetlands, lining the navigation. Kingfishers often hide in the artificial sandbanks. The rural, more meandering course continues past Hardmead Lock (No 3), and Stanstead Lock (No 4), to reach Rye House. The 15th-century mansion of the same name is no longer standing, but the surviving gatehouse, with its 12 gargoyles, is worth a visit on the north bank. This stop pairs well with a break for refreshments at the waterside Rye House pub, where you can refill water bottles and use the facilities.

The usual nature sounds are interfered with roaring engines in Hoddesdon. It is the Rye House Kart Raceway, where Lewis Hamilton first got behind the wheel. Another prominent feature is the Rye House Power Station with its three metal towers. It explains the many giant pylons along this stretch.

The River Stort joins the Lee Navigation at the junction of Feildes Weir Lock (No 5). This point also marks the start of the Lower Lea. The scenery is pleasant, with rolling countryside and colourful canal boats. En route to Broxbourne, portage

TOP Rye House Gatehouse.

LEFT A well-earned break at The Rye House pub.

OPPOSITE It's fun spotting quirky boat names on the water.

at Dobbs Weir Lock (No 6), and finally at Carthagena Lock (No 7). Watch out for the anglers casting their lines, fishing is popular here. Be considerate and, whenever safe, move to the middle of the channel to avoid disturbing them when you pass.

The commuter town of Broxbourne is the final destination of this paddle. Pass under Bridge No 51 by the Crown pub on the south bank, then hang a right at Bridge No 50 to enter Mill Stream. Ignore the 'No entry' sign – it only applies to powered craft. Get off the water before the Old Mill Retreat Café. The Lee Valley Canoe Cycle and Riverside Chalet exit points are reserved for their guests only. For your convenience, there are public toilets at the Old Mill and Meadows before you wrap up the adventure.

Paddle provider

- **Herts Canoe Club** – hertscanoeclub.org

Linking route

- 31 Broxbourne to Ponders End (Lee Navigation)

Wildlife highlight

Kingfisher (*Alcedo atthis*)
A bird very much part of the scene along the Lee Navigation is the elusive kingfisher. Blink and you'll miss it. You have to be paying attention to catch a flash of sparkling blue as it zips from the undergrowth to a new perch, always on the lookout for its next fishy snack.

Tuck in

There are several waterside pubs conveniently dotted along the route, such as the Saracens Head in Ware, Jolly Fisherman in Stanstead St Margarets, Rye House and The Fish and Eels in Hoddesdon and The Crown in Broxbourne. The towpath follows the paddle throughout and there are benches for those who prefer to bring their own snacks and drinks.

NEED TO KNOW

■ The Canal & River Trust is the navigation authority on the River Lee Navigation. A small craft licence is required, also covered by Paddle UK membership.

■ Naming conventions vary across maps. Often 'Lee' refers to the artificial navigation and 'Lea' to the natural river.

■ Lock portaging on this route is tricky. No dedicated portage points are marked, so exercise caution in finding a safe spot, considering the height and stability of the sides. Wear shoes for safety. Not recommended for canoes, kayaks or solo paddlers unless comfortable entering the water from high edges.

■ The Lee Navigation is a canalised river, but it is still subject to changes in current and water level after heavy rain. Check RiverApp for flow rate.

31 BROXBOURNE TO PONDERS END LEE NAVIGATION

A pleasant one-way paddle adventure from Broxbourne to Ponders End in Enfield, North London, along the Lee Navigation. This route alternates between rural tranquillity and urban scenery as it passes through the Lee Valley Regional Park. Expect a mixture of countryside, urban green spaces, nature reserves and lakes. Seven lock portages add a fun challenge, each one a great spot to rest and chat with interesting canal characters.

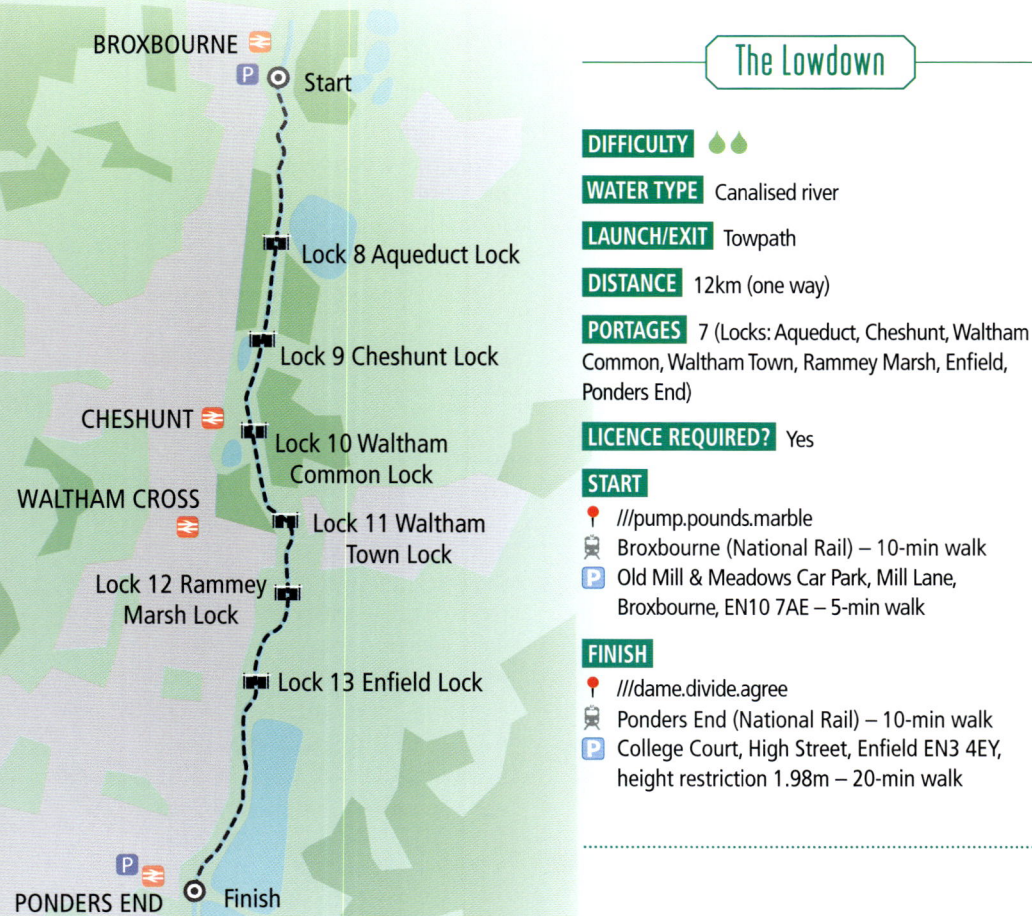

The Lowdown

DIFFICULTY ●●

WATER TYPE Canalised river

LAUNCH/EXIT Towpath

DISTANCE 12km (one way)

PORTAGES 7 (Locks: Aqueduct, Cheshunt, Waltham Common, Waltham Town, Rammey Marsh, Enfield, Ponders End)

LICENCE REQUIRED? Yes

START
- ///pump.pounds.marble
- Broxbourne (National Rail) – 10-min walk
- Old Mill & Meadows Car Park, Mill Lane, Broxbourne, EN10 7AE – 5-min walk

FINISH
- ///dame.divide.agree
- Ponders End (National Rail) – 10-min walk
- College Court, High Street, Enfield EN3 4EY, height restriction 1.98m – 20-min walk

CANALS

A brief history

The Thames is not the only river in London. One of its major tributaries, the River Lea, together with its canalised counterpart, the Lee Navigation, was always London's working river. It was a crucial but under-recognised artery for London's historical and economic development. This waterway carried grain, provided drinking water and even played a role in making explosives. You can visit the former Royal Gunpowder Mills in Waltham Abbey.

With the decline in canal trade, the Lee Valley became derelict, earning a reputation as London's privy and backyard. In the 1960s, Lee Valley Regional Park was created as a green lung for London, Essex and Hertfordshire. Industrial sites, scrapyards and gravel pits were transformed into spaces for recreation, sport and nature. The 4,050-ha park follows the course of the waterway.

The paddle

Start the paddle adventure in the leafy Hertfordshire town of Broxbourne, easily commutable and within the TfL contactless zone. The launch spot along Mill Stream is a 10-minute walk from the station, just past the Old Mill Retreat Café. Find a safe place to set off and avoid areas reserved for Lee Valley Canoe Cycle. Once on the water, pass under the railway tracks and Bridge No 50 before turning right on to the main channel of the Lee Navigation. Head south for a scenic paddle.

At Kings Weir, the natural River Lea leaves the Navigation. Keep to the right to stay on the canal. From here, the waterway becomes artificially straighter. The route includes seven portages, starting at Aqueduct Lock (No 8). The lock is named after the Small River Lea, which crosses the channel here.

ABOVE A perfect day for a paddle.

BELOW Tranquillity on the canal, so close to London.

LEFT The paddle crew in sync.

BELOW Another portage, another adventure.

The scenery is rural. There are lakes, wetlands, parks and reserves formed from old gravel pits all around. Due to the considerable number of glasshouses, Lee Valley is sometimes described as the cucumber capital of England. Portage at Cheshunt Lock (No 9). Soon after, hidden behind the Cheshunt Visitor Moorings, lies the Herts Young Mariners Base and the town of 'Chez-unt'.

Portage at the next two Waltham locks, Waltham Common (No 10) and Waltham Town (No 11). If you fancy a spin on an Olympic course, the iconic Lee Valley White Water Centre is between these locks on the right-hand side, past Bridge No 44. The navigation here is also the boundary between the Hertfordshire town of Waltham Cross to the west and the Essex town of Waltham Abbey to the east.

The section that follows is more industrial. The hum of traffic when paddling under Bridge No 42 carrying the A121 reminds you that London is not far. Crossing under Bridge No 40A with a steady stream of traffic on the M25 above may feel like the final farewell to rural tranquillity, but the banks are still overgrown and lush.

The fifth portage of the route is at Rammey Marsh Lock (No 12). There is a café across the bridge for a quick drink and facilities. Nice patio for those sunny days, too. After getting back on the water, keep to the right again when the navigation splits. This serene stretch is popular with walkers and cyclists. You might also see model planes flying overhead from the nearby Enfield Model Flying Club. The right bank often fills with colourful narrowboats puttering in and out.

Pylons and power lines pave the way along the canal as you reach Enfield Lock

ABOVE Visiting Herts Young Mariners in Cheshunt.

(No 13). You have now officially arrived in London – Enfield being the northernmost London borough. The red-brick building facing to the lock is a former toll office. Exit the water and take care with portaging, it is a longer walk and involves crossing a bridge. Spot the Bookswap box on the way?

As you near the end of the route, you are paddling between an industrial corridor along the west and King George V Reservoir on the east bank. It is one of the reservoirs supplying drinking water to London. Get off the water at Ponders End Lock (No 14). This is your final portage to complete the adventure.

Linking route

- 30 Hertford to Broxbourne (Lee Navigation)

Tuck in

- **Broxbourne**: Old Mill Retreat Café.
- **Along the route**, The River Garden at Rammey Marsh Lock, The Greyhound and The Navigation Inn in Enfield.

Paddle providers

- **Lee Valley Canoe Cycle** – lvcc.biz
- **Herts Young Mariners Base Outdoor Centre** – hymb.com
- **Lee Valley White Water Centre** – better.org.uk/lee-valley

NEED TO KNOW

■ The Canal & River Trust is the navigation authority on the Lee Navigation. A small craft licence is required, also covered by Paddle UK membership.

■ Naming conventions vary across maps. Usually, 'Lee' is used when referring to the artificial navigation and 'Lea' when referring to the natural river.

■ Angling is very popular, mind the lines.

■ Not recommended for canoes, kayaks or solo paddlers unless comfortable exiting and entering the water from high edges when portaging.

32 PONDERS END TO TOTTENHAM HALE LEE NAVIGATION

Paddle through the lower reaches of the Lee Navigation as it cuts through the North London neighbourhoods of Enfield, Chingford, Edmonton and Tottenham. This 6.5km route is perfect for wildlife spotting and bankside conversations. Enjoy the rural backdrop of the navigation, electricity pylons, liveaboard houseboats and open spaces of Lee Valley Regional Park. Despite the realities of urban life present along the route, there is an unexpected tranquillity. You find beauty in the resilience of nature coexisting with industry. Reaching Tottenham Hale after three portages, beer lovers will appreciate the craft beer scene with several local breweries.

The Lowdown

DIFFICULTY
WATER TYPE Canal/canalised river
LAUNCH/EXIT Towpath
DISTANCE 6.5km (one way)
PORTAGES 2 (Locks: Pickett's, Stonebridge)
LICENCE REQUIRED? Yes

START
- ///dame.divide.agree
- Ponders End (National Rail) – 10-min walk
- College Court, High Street, Enfield EN3 4EY, height restriction 1.98m – 20-min walk

FINISH
- ///bless.float.dimes (1)
- ///forum.talent.dozed (2)
- Tottenham Hale (1) (Victoria Line, National Rail) – 10-min walk
- Stonebridge Lock Car Park (2), Watermead Way, London, N17 0XD – free

A brief history

The Lee Valley map is speckled with blue – there are 13 reservoirs in the Lee Valley Reservoir Chain. Along this route, the tall grassy embankment to the east conceals the Chingford Reservoirs. Comprising the King George V (1912) and William Girling (1951) reservoirs, this is one of London's most extensive open water habitats. Now managed by Thames Water, the reservoirs store around 29,000 megalitres of water, enough for 11,600 Olympic pools, and provide vital habitat for wetland birds. Water from the River Lea and New River (see route 30) settles

ABOVE Pylons are a constant companion on this route.

here. Before reaching North London taps, the water undergoes a treatment process at Coppermills Water Treatment Works. It gets filtered, ozonated and disinfected. But managing London's water is not just about supply. It is also about predicting where and when water is needed. During COVID-19 lockdowns, with offices empty and people at home, usage shifted unexpectedly.

The paddle This paddle starts in Ponders End in Enfield, on the northern perimeter of London. Launch from the east bank just below Lock No 14, Ponders End Lock. The marina opposite has a string of brightly painted narrowboats moored up. Head downstream, leaving the lock behind you, and paddle past Camden Town Brewery on your right. There is no public taproom here, but you can book on to brewery tours.

Towering pylons and power lines tail the navigation. Continue past the greenery of Lee Valley golf course and the camping site in Edmonton. For a next-level urban SUP adventure, perhaps an overnight stay in one of their pods?

- Start
- PONDERS END
- Chingford Reservoirs
- Lock 15 Pickett's Lock
- EDMONTON
- CHINGFORD
- NORTHUMBERLAND PARK
- Lock 16 Stonebridge Lock
- WALTHMAMSTOW
- Lock 17 Tottenham Lock
- Finish
- TOTTENHAM HALE

LEFT Another portage but still smiling.

ABOVE A lock with a nickname.

BELOW Al fresco lunch.

RIGHT Paddling and chatting.

Chingford Reservoirs is the first in a series of water storage basins that accompany you throughout the route on the east side. These reservoirs are typically hidden behind raised grassy embankments, but on a map you can see the substantial blue area they and the flood plains occupy. This is where some of London's drinking water comes from.

The first portage is at Pickett's Lock (No 15). It is affectionally known as Alfie's Lock in honour of the legendary lock keeper who welcomed Bounty bars in exchange for a safe passage. On clear days, you may spot some familiar London landmarks from here.

The industrial zone on the west side is a waste management site. Edmonton EcoPark deals with North London's growing volumes of rubbish. Paddle under the dark shadow

cast by Bridge No 28, which is a cluster of concrete crossings carrying the roaring North Circular above. Congrats, you have now passed the halfway point.

On the far-right side, the old Tottenham IKEA has been converted into a massive North London cultural venue. Drumsheds sees some big names and therefore, big crowds. Paddle through the green open space of Tottenham Marshes, stretching on both sides, to arrive at Stonebridge Lock (No 16). There is a water point here, facilities if you have the Canal & River Trust key and a lovely waterside café.

The final leg to Tottenham is the shortest stretch between two locks, or a 'pound' in canal lingo, on the Lee Navigation. Exit the water at Tottenham Lock (No 17), and walk to Bridge No 24 to access the ramp on to Ferry Lane. If you are heading in the direction of the station, don't miss the huge street art canvases in the side streets off Broad Lane.

Linking routes

- 31 Broxbourne to Ponders End (Lee Navigation)
- 33 Clapton to Hackney Wick (Lee Navigation)

Tuck in

- **Enfield**: The Navigation Inn.
- **Along the route**, Stonebridge Lock Waterside Cafe.
- **Tottenham Hale**: Ferry Boat Inn, several brewery taprooms, such as Beavertown, Pressure Drop and Mother Kelly's, some with food stalls.

NEED TO KNOW

■ The Canal & River Trust is the navigation authority on the Lee Navigation. A small craft licence is required, also covered by Paddle UK membership.

■ Naming conventions vary across maps. Usually, 'Lee' is used when referring to the artificial navigation and 'Lea' when referring to the natural river.

■ Not recommended for canoes, kayaks or solo paddlers unless comfortable exiting and entering the water from high edges when portaging.

33 CLAPTON TO HACKNEY WICK LEE NAVIGATION

'Set off at the Princess of Wales?' is a common opener in the East London paddlers' group. This much-loved route from the Clapton riverside pub down to Hackney Wick and back covers 6.5km and is lock-free. It's perfect for a leisurely social paddle, letting you soak in the laid-back feel of Hackney Marshes and the urban buzz along the Wick's enviable canal-side strip. It's like Amsterdam, but better. Plus, it's one of the rare inner London paddle destinations with parking close by.

The Lowdown

DIFFICULTY

WATER TYPE Canal/canalised river

LAUNCH/EXIT Towpath

DISTANCE 6.5km (round trip)

PORTAGES 0

LICENCE REQUIRED? Yes

START/FINISH
- ///excuse.posts.bond
- Clapton (Weaver, National Rail); Lea Bridge (National Rail) – 15-min walk
- Lee Valley Ice Centre, Lea Bridge Road, London E10 7QL, height restriction 2m – 8-min walk

A brief history

The 3km length of the Lee Navigation spanning between Lea Bridge Road bridge and the Old Ford Lock is called the Hackney Cut. It is one of the several bypasses built on to the winding natural channel of the River Lea in the 18th century. For years after, this grid of waterways kept on powering the capital's industrial growth. Once the industries closed, Lower Lea Valley turned into derelict wasteland.

The London 2012 Olympics promised to bring social, economic and environmental improvements to this little-known backyard of London. Lee Valley Regional Park is now a green playground, home to wildlife and nature, with the Lee Navigation and River Lea running through it.

The paddle

Launch from the towpath in front of the Princess of Wales pub in Clapton, on the eastern edge of the London Borough of Hackney. Even with the congested Lea Bridge Road, it is a surprisingly serene spot with an off-the-

CANALS

ABOVE Start and finish at The Princess of Wales.

beaten-track vibe, popular with pub-goers, walkers and cyclists. It is like a secret back door to inner London.

Start your journey south to Hackney Wick. The pylons that dominated the horizon on other sections of the Lee Navigation have received the Olympic makeover. All the cables are buried underground here.

A 'No access' sign on the left guides you to paddle past Lea Bridge Weir, where the navigation and natural river part ways. Excess water passes over the weir into the River Lea, meandering to the east. It won't meet the canal again until Old Ford Lock (see route 29). Between the two waterways

LEFT Old Ford Lock is the halfway point of the route.

RIGHT Bridges in Hackney Wick.

BOTTOM LEFT Paddleboarding on Hackney Cut.

BOTTOM RIGHT Words to live by.

is Middlesex Filter Beds, today a nature reserve. The granite blocks are an art installation.

Glide through the bubble barrier in front of Bridge No 17A, Walthamstow Crossover Bridge. This clever system improves water quality by collecting debris and aerating the water without restricting navigation. The towpath changes sides here, from right to left. The name of the bridge stems from the

old days when horses towing boats would have to cross over. It was more economical to have the towpath on one side only.

Follow the gentle curve of the canal before the cut starts its straight course down. Liveaboard boats of all shapes, sizes and conditions line the water. The Canal & River Trust has introduced 'No Mooring Zones' in recent years, but boaters can moor for up to 14 days in most places along the Lower Lea.

Hackney Marshes on the left backs on to the water. With more than 80 football pitches, cheery sounds fill the air, especially on Sundays. The left bank remains green until Bridge No 14, but urban realities peek through with random abandoned household items, graffiti and traffic noise.

On the final approach to Hackney Wick, familiar landmarks of London are firmly in your sights. Paddle towards the Olympic Stadium and the red ArcelorMittal Orbit, the UK's tallest sculpture. You'll pass a lively canal-side strip with ample al-fresco drinking and dining options, plus free activities such as big screen films and sports at Here East.

Leaving the Hertford Union Junction – the entrance to the canal that shortcuts to Regent's Canal – to your right, continue to the halfway point of Old Ford Lock, Lock No 19. Consider taking a break at one of Hackney Wick's establishments before returning to Clapton.

Linking routes
- 29 Limehouse Loop (Lee Navigation)
- 32 Ponders End to Tottenham Hale (Lee Navigation)

Tuck in
- **Clapton**: The Princess of Wales and The Anchor & Hope.
- **Hackney Wick**: Impressive line-up of waterside cafés, terraces and restaurants, too many to list.

Paddle provider
- **Moo Canoes** – moocanoes.com

NEED TO KNOW

■ The Canal & River Trust is the navigation authority on the Lee Navigation. A small craft licence is required, also covered by Paddle UK membership.

■ Check the parking rules at Lee Valley Ice Centre. At the time of writing, you can get up to three hours of free parking if you spend £5 in their café.

■ The Hackney Wick stretch suffers from thick duckweed coverage in the warmer months.

OTHER WATERWAYS

The final section offers a varied selection of seven routes. Some right in the heart of London, others a little further out, but all easy to reach.

For an inner-city paddle, head to Royal Victoria Dock, where you get to paddle against a backdrop of cable cars, Canary Wharf and London City Airport. There is even a beach. Or swap the hustle and bustle for the calm of West Reservoir in Hackney. Perfect for working on your paddle skills or unwinding with a SUP yoga class.

Looking for a bit more adventure? The River Mole in Surrey is swift and exciting, while the Jubilee River is so peaceful you would never guess it is actually a flood relief channel for Maidenhead, Windsor and Eton. If you are up for a long-distance challenge, the River Wey and Godalming Navigations take you through rural scenery before delivering you on to the Thames at Shepperton. And then there are two routes along the Basingstoke Canal, a beauty in any season, but simply unmissable in autumn.

Planning
Check the individual routes for planning details.

LEFT 'All the Wey' is a 33km paddle route.

OPPOSITE Ready to launch.

34 CROOKHAM WHARF TO COLT HILL BASINGSTOKE

Easily accessible by car from London, this 17km round trip from Crookham Village to Colt Hill on the Basingstoke Canal offers a scenic, lock-free paddle through Hampshire's unspoilt countryside. Expect peace and quiet, just the odd trip boat passing by. Suitable for all levels, the route meanders through pockets of woods and heathland dotted with old brick arch bridges and military structures. It is often a safe countryside alternative to drive to when other waterways are in flood. Whether you are chasing autumn's changing colours or summer's blooms, this paddle never fails to deliver.

The Lowdown

DIFFICULTY

WATER TYPE Canal

LAUNCH/EXIT Towpath

DISTANCE 17km (round trip)

PORTAGES 0

LICENCE REQUIRED? Yes

START/FINISH
- ///custodian.convert.tributes
- Fleet or Winchfield (National Rail) – 15-min taxi
- Crookham Wharf Car Park, Crookham Village, Fleet GU51 5SZ – free

ABOVE Paddling under a canopy of trees.

A brief history

The Basingstoke Canal was built in the late 18th century to transport agricultural produce from Hampshire to London. The canal fell into disrepair as it never quite met its industrial goals, and after years of neglect, Hampshire and Surrey county councils took over in the 1970s, with the Basingstoke Canal Authority managing it day-to-day. A major conservation project in the 1990s dredged the channel of mud and silt and restored the

OTHER WATERWAYS 177

locks and bridges. Now designated an SSSI for its unique aquatic plant life, the canal still faces challenges like water shortages and aging infrastructure. These have led to restrictions on the number of motorised boats and lock usage – all the more reason for paddlers to enjoy this carefully restored rural waterway.

The paddle

Launch from the Crookham Wharf car park, right by the canal. A sign warns that overnight parking is not allowed. If you arrive and find the gate closed, the Canal & River Trust key can be used for access. Set off to your right, upstream, leaving Chequers Bridge behind. Cruise under a canopy of trees that create an intimate, secluded atmosphere, like you have entered a world all your own. Time? It ticks at a more leisurely pace here.

As you paddle on, two moss-covered concrete cylinders stick out of the canal. There will be more along the way, including pyramid-shaped dragon's teeth. They look like mooring points but are in fact tank traps from the Second World War. You may also make out the occasional pillbox hiding in the canal-side undergrowth. These wartime structures now sit quietly in the peaceful setting of the canal.

The next section takes you through

ABOVE Launching from Crookham Wharf.

pockets of woodland, the route meandering through Coxmoore Wood. Carrying on upstream, the scenery shifts between the old brick arch bridges – Double Bridge and Blacksmith's Bridge – from parkland to the historic woodlands of Dogmersfield. Towering pines and a massive rhododendron wall greet you at Arch Plantation, where purple blooms in early summer fill the air with a sweet scent.

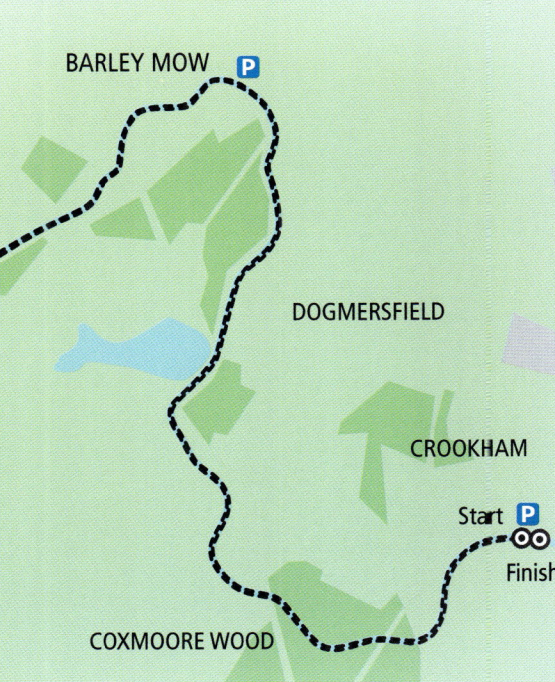

LEFT Stone arch bridge.

BELOW It is a spa day.

OPPOSITE Summer paddle.

Power lines and pylons briefly break the charm, but Barley Mow Bridge soon restores that quintessential English character. It is a picture-perfect spot, especially if you catch the Accessible Boating Association's narrowboat, *Dawn*, drifting by.

Further along is a thatched country house with a life-size horse statue in the garden. It looks very realistic from the canal viewpoint. Make your way through a series of Grade II listed bridges, named after local farms and families: Stacey's Farm Bridge, Baseley's Bridge, Sprat's Hatch Bridge and Sandy Hill Bridge.

Next you are paddling along the grounds of Dogmersfield House on your left, the estate turned into a hotel. There is a lake as well, not visible from the water, but the hotel's narrowboat *Louise II* often makes an appearance, leisurely cruising up and down the canal. Pass the Broad Oak feeder stream, one of the canal's sparse water sources. The inlet is formed like a little pool and on a hot day it is just the spot for a quick dip of toes.

The last section keeps in line with the rural nature of the waterway. As you approach the halfway point, the canal comes to life with kayakers, canoes and rowboats, especially in summer, when Galleon Marine is busy renting out boats. The annual Odiham Raft Race, usually held the first Sunday in September, is a local event worth checking out. Two more bridges

– Broad Oak and Odiham Bypass – mark the final stretch before arriving at Odiham Wharf (see route 35). Past Colt Hill Bridge, treat yourself to a break at the Waterwitch pub's canal-side garden before setting off on the return leg.

Linking route
- 35 Colt Hill to Greywell Tunnel (Basingstoke)

Wildlife highlight
Rhododendron (*Rhododendron ponticum*) The flowering rhododendrons along the Dogmersfield stretch are a stunning early spring display. However, their beauty comes at a cost. Introduced from Asia in Victorian times to grace grand estates, the ponticum variety has become invasive. It overhangs the canal, blocks sunlight for native water species and threatens the ecosystem that earned the canal its SSSI status. The Basingstoke Canal Authority and the landowners must now manage these floral invaders to protect the canal's biodiversity.

Tuck in
- **Crookham Wharf**: The Exchequer, a few minutes' walk from the launch point.
- **Along the route**: The Barley Mow in Winchfield, The Waterwitch (no direct access from the canal) and coffee trailer Hettie at Colt Hill Wharf.

Paddle providers
- **Galleon Marine** – galleonmarine.co.uk
- **Paddle SUP Company** – paddlesupcompany.com
- **Basingstoke & Deane Canoe Club** – badpaddlers.org

NEED TO KNOW

■ The Basingstoke Canal Authority (BCA) manages the canal. A licence is required for paddling, which you can buy from the BCA. They offer daily, weekly or annual options. The Paddle UK 'On The Water' membership also covers the canal. The ranger team regularly checks licences.

■ The Basingstoke Canal often provides a safe alternative when other waterways are in flood. The canal is fully man-made, it does not have a natural river feed and its levels are carefully monitored 24/7, 365 days. Navigation updates – facebook.com/basingstokecanal.

35 COLT HILL TO GREYWELL TUNNEL BASINGSTOKE

Looking for a quick nature fix less than an hour from London? The Basingstoke Canal in Hampshire is an excellent, beginner-friendly alternative. This peaceful lock-free route in Odiham is straight out of a fairy tale – royal castle ruin, bat-filled tunnel and fish swimming in clear water. In summer, the canal is all lush greenery and colourful blooms, while autumn paints the scene with warm hues reflecting off the still water. In winter and spring, the Basingstoke Canal offers a safe, sheltered setting. With free parking close to the canal, it is as convenient as it is picturesque.

The Lowdown

DIFFICULTY

WATER TYPE Canal

LAUNCH/EXIT Towpath

DISTANCE 7km (round trip)

PORTAGES 0

LICENCE REQUIRED? Yes

START/FINISH
- ///revisits.patrol.shippers
- Winchfield (National Rail) – 15-min taxi
- Colt Hill Wharf car park, Odiham RG29 1AL – free

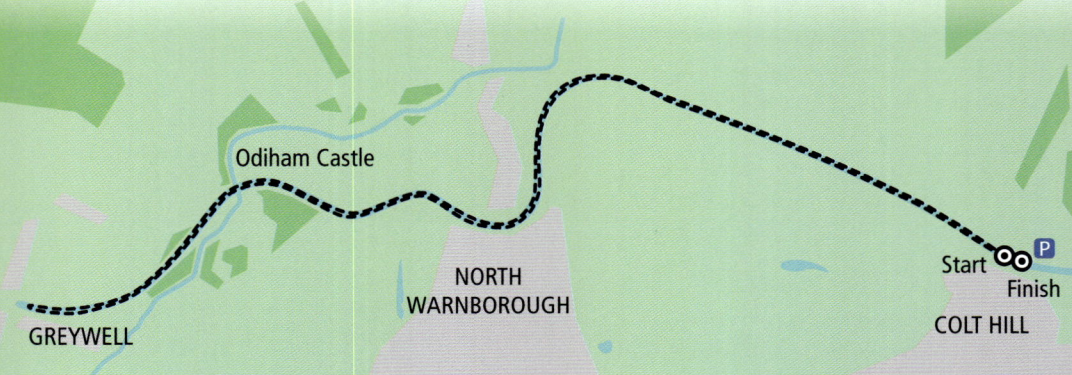

A brief history

The Basingstoke Canal, stretching from Basingstoke to the junction of the Wey Navigation in Woodham, opened in 1794. The 60km canal was dug, complete with construction of towing paths, 30 locks, 52 bridges, 10 wharves, 4 lock houses, 2 aqueducts and a 1km tunnel. All this by hand! The goal was to boost trade between Hampshire and London, but the canal struggled commercially and quickly fell into disrepair. Over the years, it witnessed bankruptcies, deception and even the literal collapse of the Greywell Tunnel. The start point, Colt Hill Wharf, was one of the wharves where cargo was loaded and unloaded on its way to and from London. Today, 50km of the Basingstoke Canal are navigable. As a Site of Special Scientific Interest, it is a haven for a restricted number of powered boats as well as paddlers, walkers and anglers.

The paddle

The large free car park at Colt Hill in Odiham is a few minutes' walk from the canal towpath. You arrive at a hub for canal leisure with a trip boat mooring, boatyard, narrowboat and small boat hire, canoe club and SUP company. Hop on your craft opposite Galleon Marine, heading right and under the arch of Colt Hill Bridge. Paddle past *John Pinkerton* Canal Cruises, named for the original contractor of the canal. The John Pinkerton II is one of the few larger boats you may encounter on this stretch. Give them a wave. Skippered by volunteers, all proceeds go to help maintain the canal.

Continue past the gardens of the Waterwitch pub, stretching to the water's edge. The towpath trails the canal on your right. For the next kilometre, the navigation is arrow straight. Trees line the canal, leaning towards the water, creating a tunnel-like effect with open fields beyond.

After Lodge Copse Bridge, travel along

ABOVE Visiting the historic Odiham Castle.

the canal as it bends left. Watch for the sluice on the right, especially after heavy rain. Paddle under another brick arch bridge, Swan Bridge. The pub it was named after is no longer there, but if you want to top up on supplies, there is a petrol station just up the road to the right. The next bridge is the North Warnborough lifting beam bridge, which is electrically operated for boats, but paddlers get to duck under it. Mind your head!

Take a break to explore the ruins of Odiham Castle, also known as King John's Castle. No better spot for a picnic than the remains of a 13th-century royal hunting lodge. Check out the information panels for a bit of history. There is even a Magna Carta link (see route 04).

Once back on the water, the buoys at the turning basin mark the end of boat

LEFT Peaceful waters.

BELOW Taking a break at Odiham Castle.

RIGHT Mind your head.

navigation. The final adventurous stretch to Greywell Tunnel is open for paddlers, conditions permitting. It is a nature reserve. There is no canal maintenance here, so access may be blocked by weeds or low water. With water from springs in the tunnel and no traffic stirring up the bottom silt to the surface, enjoy the crystal-clear waters, with fish swimming under your board. Paddle past a former lock to reach the eastern portal of Greywell Tunnel. Keep your visit quiet and respectful. The tunnel collapsed years ago and is now closed off as a winter bat roost.

Retrace your paddle strokes back to Colt Hill Wharf.

Linking route

- 34 Crookham Wharf to Colt Hill (Basingstoke)

Wildlife highlight

Soprano pipistrelle bat
(*Pipistrellus pygmaeus*)
Out of the 18 bat species found in the UK, the soprano pipistrelle is one of the most common. To encounter these small flying mammals with brown fur and black wings, you have to be out paddling around sunset in summer, when bats go hunting over the canal. If you are serious about it, bring a bat detector to pick up their ultrasonic calls that are too high for the human ear.

The Basingstoke Canal is a buffet for these nocturnal predators, rich with midges and mosquitoes. Using echolocation, bats

navigate and catch their prey, consuming as many as three thousand insects a night. Come winter, they retreat to Greywell Tunnel – a cool, humid refuge for up to ten thousand hibernating bats from several species.

Tuck in

Bring your own snacks for this route. Close to the start/end point are the canal-side Waterwitch pub and the converted horsebox coffee bar Hettie at Galleon Marine. The Fox and Goose is not far from Greywell Tunnel.

Paddle providers

- Galleon Marine – galleonmarine.co.uk
- Paddle SUP Company – paddlesupcompany.com
- Basingstoke & Deane Canoe Club – badpaddlers.org

NEED TO KNOW

■ The Basingstoke Canal is an independent waterway. The Basingstoke Canal Authority (BCA) manages the canal on behalf of the canal's joint owners, Surrey and Hampshire county councils. An unpowered boat licence is required for paddling and can be bought from the BCA. Licence options include daily, weekly or annual. They are regularly checked. The Paddle UK 'On The Water' membership also covers the use of Basingstoke Canal.

■ Navigation updates are provided on the Basingstoke Canal Facebook page – facebook.com/basingstokecanal.

36 GODALMING TO SHEPPERTON WEY NAVIGATIONS

'All the Wey', because there is something undeniably satisfying about conquering an entire waterway. This 33km route is a beauty. Starting in Godalming, paddle through Surrey's stockbroker belt along the Wey and Godalming Navigations. Launch early, stop for lunch in Send, grab a drink in Pyrford and finish just past Weybridge at Shepperton Lock on the Thames. Expect a mix of rural tranquillity, wildlife, history, a touch of urban charm and even some unexpected street art. With 16 locks and flood gates, there is plenty of portaging and ample opportunities to choose your favourite lock. Papercourt, anyone?

The Lowdown

DIFFICULTY

WATER TYPE River navigation and river

LAUNCH/EXIT Riverbank

DISTANCE 33km (one way)

PORTAGES 14–16 (Locks: Catteshall, Unstead, St Catherine's, Millmead, Stoke, Bowers, Triggs, Worsfold Gates, Papercourt, Newark, Walsham Gates, Pyrford, New Haw, Coxes, Weybridge Town, Thames)

LICENCE REQUIRED? Yes

START
- ///verge.divisions.doctor
- Godalming (National Rail) – 10-min walk
- Crown Court Car Park, 41 The Burys, Godalming GU7 1HR – 5-min walk

FINISH
- ///guards.digit.incomes
- Shepperton (National Rail) – 10-min taxi
- Shepperton Lock Car Park, Towpath, Shepperton TW17 9LQ – free

A brief history

The Wey River flows 140km from two sources in Hampshire and West Sussex, joining the Thames in Weybridge. Back in the day, Wey Valley prospered with agriculture. The steady flow of the river powered 22 mills at its peak, producing everything from flour to gunpowder.

In the 17th century, local landowner Sir Richard Weston, whose mansion this route passes, envisioned a navigable waterway linking Guildford to the Thames. By cutting through the river's natural meanders and constructing locks and weirs, the 26km Wey Navigation opened in 1653. Over time, it

OTHER WATERWAYS 185

ABOVE A magnificent tree.

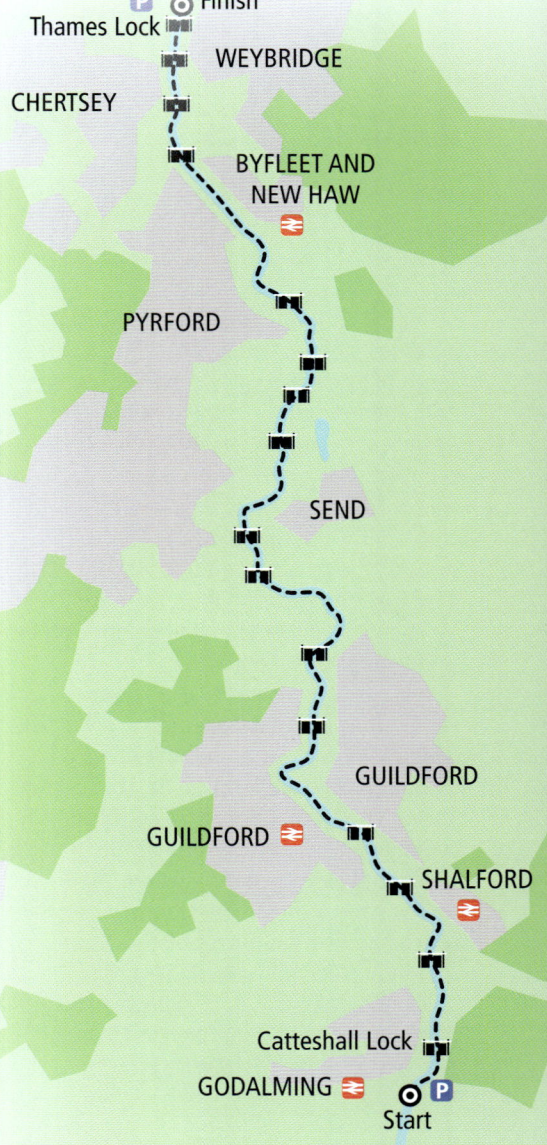

atmosphere of Farncombe Boat House. Hire boats coming and going, varying navigational skill adding to the entertainment. Mind the weir on the right before Unstead Lock (No 15). The Wey and Arun joins at Gun's Mouth junction, but this stretch is unnavigable, even for paddlers. After the railway bridge, stay clear of the Riff Raff weir below St Catherine's Lock (No 14).

became Britain's first commercially viable canalised river, long before the canal age. In 1764, the Godalming Navigation extended the route another 6km upstream.

The Wey and Godalming Navigations have been owned and managed by the National Trust since 1964. The navigations alternate between running parallel to the natural river and using canalised sections of it.

The paddle
Nestled along the Wey, Godalming has a nice country town feel. Launch at Phillips Memorial Park, conveniently near the station and car park, just upstream of Godalming Wharf, the head of navigation for powered boats. From here, paddle downstream along the waterside meadows of Lammas Lands.

The upper reaches of the Wey capture rural Surrey at its finest – wooded hills, grazing cattle, pretty bridges and lock keepers' cottages. There are four locks on the Godalming Navigation. After portaging at Catteshall Lock (No 16), enjoy the

ABOVE The quiet beauty of a lock cut.

RIGHT The paddle crew.

Approaching Guildford, the landscape becomes steeper. Paddle past the golden sands of St Catherine's Hill, which leads from the footbridge to the chapel ruins. Despite the 'Danger' warning, the bridge is popular for jumping into the water. This was once a ford on the Pilgrims' Way, with a ferry crossing the river. Follow the signs as the navigation takes a sharp left past Guildford Rowing Club, ending at Millmead Lock (No 13), the final lock on the Godalming Navigation.

You are now on the Wey Navigation. Paddle through Guildford town centre. The riverside is very urban but overlooked by the medieval Guildford Castle. This is Lewis Carroll land – there is an 'Alice Through The Looking-Glass' statue in the castle grounds, sadly not visible from the water. The Town Bridge carries the cobblestoned high street, which shows off a mix of historic buildings, Guildhall clock and excellent shopping.

Dapdune Wharf is next and worth a stop. Originally one of the first wharves on the Wey and a boatyard, the site now hosts the National Trust visitor centre with exhibits, tearoom and picnic areas. Every September, Wey River Festival brings boaters and public alike to the wharf.

Continue your paddle under the Dapdune railway bridge. The left bank between here and the A25 bridge trails Woodbridge Meadows. Spot any sculptures?

Paddle through rural scenery, portaging at Stoke Lock (No 12) and Bowers Lock (No 11). You may hear the hum of traffic from the nearby A3. Below Bowers, the backwater joins the main navigation channel, which takes a sharp right turn after the lock. The route sweeps around the grounds of Sutton Place, the 17th-century mansion built for Sir Richard Weston. Former owner J. Paul Getty installed a telephone box on the grounds to make sure guests paid for their own calls. He was a billionaire.

Triggs Lock (No 10) with its gingerbread cottage is the halfway point of the route. As a sign points out, the next canal-side pub and garden is the New Inn in Send, about a kilometre downstream. Perfect for lunch or a drink. First pass Worsfold Gates (No 9), left open unless flooding, and follow the navigation winding through backwaters and meadows.

Two portages remain to get to the flint ruins of Newark Priory. At Papercourt Lock (No 8), portage right, past the tumbling bay. At Newark Lock (No 7), portage on the left, cross the towpath footbridge and relaunch below. You can feel the flow picking up with the natural river and Abbey Stream joining. For the best photo opportunity in front of the Augustinian priory, take a detour up the millstream. Regrettably, in warmer months, floating pennywort may block your way. This historic monastery, now on private land, was among those dissolved by King Henry VIII.

Paddle on to Walsham Gates (No 6), where there is no drop under normal conditions. Be sure to check out the last original turf-sided lock, once common on the Wey, before continuing to Pyrford Lock (No 5). After portaging at Pyrford, cross the road carefully. The Anchor's waterside garden is pure Surrey charm and hard to resist. RHS Garden Wisley is nearby, perhaps best saved for a trip without the paddle kit.

Green canal-sides, ancient trees and a golf course guide you towards Byfleet, where the M25 briefly adds an unwelcome soundtrack. Just before the flyover, Woodham Junction connects the Wey to the Basingstoke Canal (see route 34), which used to stretch 51km to Basingstoke. The New Haw underpass feels like an open-air gallery, its concrete walls a canvas for street art, complete with artists at work.

The last four locks are just short stretches apart. At New Haw Lock (No 4), the cottage is said to be haunted by the lock keeper's wife. Portage here and take care crossing Byfleet Road to get back on the water. Coxes Lock (No 3), near Addlestone, is not far. Back in the day, Coxes Mill was the largest mill on the Wey. The finest bit of industrial architecture along the route, the buildings have been converted to flats and the mill pond is dedicated to wildlife. When portaging on the right, stay clear of the force of the water discharging on the opposite side. It's like a waterfall.

At Weybridge Town Lock (No 2), portage left, cross Addlestone Road and continue along the towpath via a footbridge. You arrive at a wharf pool where the navigation meets the natural river (see route 05) with the arched Old Wey Bridge. No prizes for guessing how the town got its name. Paddle the final kilometre to Thames Lock, soaking in the last of Wey. On one side, homes with dreamy gardens, on the other, woodland.

Keep your licence handy. Thames Lock (No 1) is the only attended lock on the Wey and checks are common. Portage left by the National Trust info hut, open the gate and follow the path through Weybridge Rowing Club to access the Thames via their pontoon. It might feel like you are intruding, but this is the designated portage. Just tread respectfully.

Launch right on to the Thames, navigating on the right-hand side as you paddle downstream. Pass Shepperton Weir on the opposite side, one of the Thames's largest and a playground for kayakers chasing the legendary Shepperton wave. Continue past Lock Island and take a left into Shepperton Lock just before the ferry crossing. Congratulations, you have completed 'All the Wey'!

ABOVE The must-have shot at Newark Priory.

ABOVE Curious cows watching the paddlers pass.

Linking routes

- 04 Windsor to Hampton Court (River Thames)
- 05 Weybridge (River Thames)

Wildlife highlight

Himalayan balsam (*Impatiens glandulifera*) Looks can be deceiving. Sometimes called poor man's orchid, those pretty pink flowers so common along the navigations are Himalayan balsam and it is a menace. Introduced from the Himalayas in the 19th century, this invasive plant crowds out native species and spreads via explosive seed-pods. Each plant can produce up to 800 seeds and scatter them over 5m. Seeds that reach the water travel downstream and spread it further. The most effective solution to tackle it is balsam bashing – pulling the weeds up before they flower in June.

Tuck in

Pack plenty of snacks and drinks to stay hydrated and energised.
- **Along the Wey**: White House, Britannia, Weyside, Guildford town centre, Dapdune Wharf café and tearoom, New Inn, Anchor, White Hart Inn, Pelican and Weybridge town centre.
- **Shepperton Lock**: The Ferry Coffee Shop and Shepperton Lock Tea Room.

Paddle providers

- **Roar Outdoor** – roaroutdoor.co.uk
- **Wey Kayak Club** – weykayak.co.uk
- Tours are done by groups like **Dittons Paddle Boarding**, **Fluid Adventures** and **Paddle Up**

NEED TO KNOW

■ The National Trust is the navigation authority for the River Wey Navigation. The towpath tails along the entire length and is also owned by the National Trust. Check out their guide for users of portable craft. A licence is required, but Paddle UK's 'On The Water' membership covers this waterway as well.

■ As a river navigation, the Wey is subject to flooding. Check the river conditions on riverweyconditionsnt.wordpress.com. Ensure the Wey flow rate and water levels are suitable for paddling on the GOV.UK site or a river app.

■ No paddling between sunset and sunrise.

■ For groups of 10 or more, an events licence is needed.

■ The Thames Lock is manned and there is a helpful National Trust information point. You may be asked for your waterways licence.

■ The final bit is on the Thames, so check gov.uk/guidance/river-thames-current-river-conditions.

OTHER WATERWAYS 189

37 MARSH LANE TO MANOR FARM JUBILEE RIVER

The Jubilee River is an artificial flood relief channel for Maidenhead, Windsor and Eton. When not operational, the Jubilee is your secret paddle spot beside the Thames. With no motorised boats, it offers a tranquil setting for a 6.5km round trip between Marsh Lane and Manor Farm weirs. You glide through reed beds and under footbridges, mostly undisturbed by traffic noise, save for a brief encounter with the M4. Expect to see herons and other birds at Dorney Wetlands. Visit in early autumn for a chance to see cygnet flight school. After your paddle, treat yourself to a sensational sandwich at The Pineapple pub.

The Lowdown

DIFFICULTY ●●
WATER TYPE River flood relief channel
LAUNCH/EXIT Riverbank
DISTANCE 6.5km
PORTAGES 0

LICENCE REQUIRED? Yes
START/FINISH
- ///double.wages.slower
- Taplow (Elizabeth Line, National Rail) – 15-min walk
- Marsh Lane Car Park, Taplow SL6 0DH – free

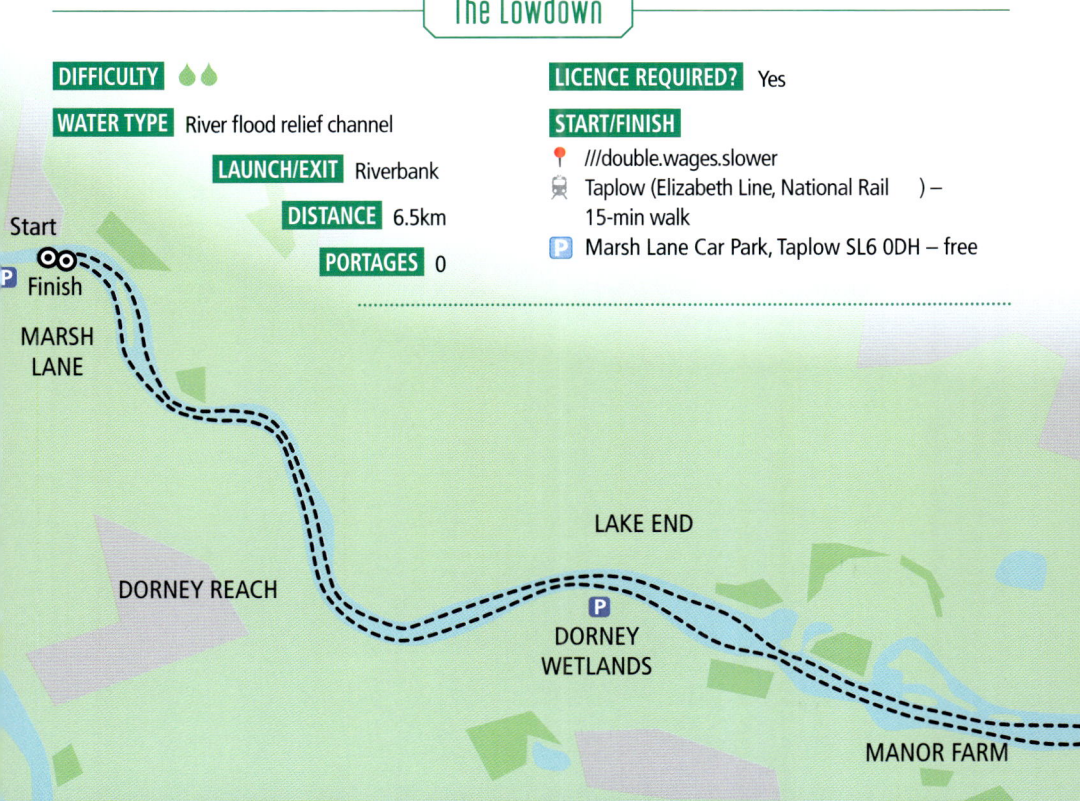

LEFT Still waters of the Jubilee River.

BELOW Curious young swans.

RIGHT Weir, the turnaround point.

A brief history

The Jubilee River is an artificial flood relief channel, constructed to reduce flood risk in the Maidenhead, Windsor and Eton areas. Opened in 2002, marking Queen Elizabeth II's Golden Jubilee, it helps protect 3,000 properties by diverting excess flow from the River Thames during flood conditions. The 11km channel starts above Boulters Lock, passes Maidenhead, Windsor and Eton and rejoins the Thames at Datchet.

Built and maintained by the Environment Agency, the channel includes five weirs to control water levels. Under normal circumstances, it carries about 10 cubic metres of water per second (cumecs).

When the Thames experiences high flows, weir gates at Taplow are gradually opened, allowing up to 180 cumecs to flow through the Jubilee.

With climate change leading to heavier and more frequent rainfall, the Jubilee River is likely to see increased use, which means fewer paddling opportunities.

The paddle

Make your way to Marsh Lane car park. The upstream side is popular with wild swimmers, emerging in their change robes. But you should head to the opposite side. Cross the road to get downstream of the weir and follow the paved footpath, shared with the National Cycle Network route. Within the greenery, a small sandy patch – safely away from the weir – provides a decent launch spot. Be cautious of the muddy, slippery banks and steep drop-off. The channel averages 4–5m deep, so be ready to get your feet wet.

Paddle downstream and leave the weir behind. It's hard to believe that the Jubilee is an artificial river. It feels so natural, meandering along reed beds and greenery, away from any development. Since it is not open to boats, it is wonderfully quiet and full of wildlife. This design was intended to replace habitats and breeding areas once lost from the Thames.

A narrow island divides the channel into two. Take either side and remember to pick the opposite one on your return. The first bridge is Glebe Close footbridge. Beyond it, you hear the hum of busy traffic from the M4. The blue direction sign for Slough is a strange contrast to the peacefulness of the Jubilee. Pass under the concrete road bridge to escape the fumes.

The next bend leads to Ashford Lane footbridge, where a heron often sits stoically on the wooden beams, unfazed by paddlers. After a few houses on the left, you reach Lake End road bridge. There is another car park on the right-hand side. Not visible from the water, between the Jubilee and the Thames, Eton College Dorney Lake is an Olympic-standard rowing and canoeing training centre. Sadly, it is not bookable for individuals. However, you can explore the parkland later. Dorney Court manor house is also located in the area, known for the first pineapple grown in England in the 17th century.

The channel widens soon, with some backwaters too shallow for paddling. Dorney Wetlands is a wildlife haven with reed beds, islands and scrapes. Keep an eye out for swans, red kites and plenty of ducks, geese and songbirds. Plus, birdwatchers with binoculars behind viewing screens.

The last bridge on this route is Manor Farm footbridge. When you see the yellow warning markers across the water before Manor Farm weir, it is time to turn around and paddle back to your starting point. Enjoy the serenity and wildlife once more on your return journey.

Wildlife highlight

Mute swan (*Cygnus olor*)
With their white plumage, S-shaped necks and orange beaks, mute swans are

ABOVE The best sandwiches ever.

among Britain's most iconic waterbirds. They begin life as fluffy grey or brown cygnets before transforming into the graceful swans that inspired Hans Christian Andersen's 'The Ugly Duckling'. The tradition of Swan Upping continues today, now a conservation practice rather than a declaration of ownership by the Crown. On the Jubilee River, swans are a common sight, particularly near Dorney Wetlands. Early autumn is peak season for cygnet flying lessons. Think frantic flapping, splashy take-offs and wobbly landings. Majestic as they are, swans are fiercely territorial, especially when breeding. When paddling near them, give a wide berth and avoid sudden movements.

Tuck in

Bring a packed lunch, snacks and drinks. For a treat after, get yourself to The Pineapple (thepineappledorney.co.uk). It is a must for any sandwich-lover, their sandwich menu is beyond impressive.

Paddle providers

- **Paddleboard Maidenhead** – paddleboardmaidenhead.uk
- **Jubilee River Riverside Centre** – jubileeriversidecentre.wordpress.com

NEED TO KNOW

- The Environment Agency (EA) manages and operates the Jubilee River flood relief channel. Strictly no entry when the Jubilee is operational as a flood defence. Unlike flood alert and flood warning messages, note that you will not be notified that a message has been issued for the Jubilee. You need to call in for information: Floodline tel. 0345 988 1188 (24-hour automated service), the reference for the Jubilee Flood Relief Channel is 215007.

- Always check the river conditions before launching – gov.uk/guidance/river-thames-current-river-conditions. The Jubilee itself is not navigable for boats, so there is no warning system. If there are stream warnings at Boulters Lock, it is likely that the Jubilee River could become operational. It is worth checking the RiverApp for gauge readings for Maidenhead at Thames and Taplow at Jubilee (normal flow 10 m^3/s).

- You need permission from the Environment Agency to paddle. Only designated access points such as Marsh Lane can be used to enter the water.

38 ESHER TO HERSHAM RIVER MOLE

An adventurous paddle for experienced paddlers on the swift River Mole, just outside London in Surrey. The route starts in serene countryside and transitions into an outing through a dense forest and lush riverbanks. Not navigable for boats, this elusive waterway offers a magical atmosphere. Natural obstacles, such as fallen trees and patches of floating pennywort, often block the route, making it impractical for those looking to clock mileage. The river flow and water levels require careful monitoring and planning. Best accessed by driving, there's a car park nearby.

The Lowdown

DIFFICULTY ●●●
WATER TYPE River
LAUNCH/EXIT Riverbank
DISTANCE 4km or shorter (return)
PORTAGES locks but there may be other obstacles requiring portage
LICENCE REQUIRED? No
START/FINISH
- ///retain.clear.hotels
- Hersham (National Rail) – 25-min walk
- West End Recreation Ground, W End Ln, Esher KT10 8NE, height restriction 2.1m – free

A brief history

Rising in West Sussex, the River Mole flows 80km into Surrey before joining the Thames at Molesey, near Hampton Court Palace. It even sneaks a peak under Gatwick Airport along the way. Some suggest the name reflects the river's mole-like behaviour, retreating into underground swallow holes during periods of low water. It is more likely, though, that the name comes from the Latin 'mola' for mill. The mills are long gone, but the river is still strong.

The Mole once flowed into the Thames at the current Hampton Court Bridge site. Now, it splits at Island Barn Reservoir. The northern branch continues as the River Mole while the southern branch becomes the Ember, but entering the Thames in a single channel. Despite historic efforts to make the Mole navigable, only the final bit to the Thames via the Ember is suitable for boats. The rest of the river? Left for recreational activities like paddling and angling.

ABOVE The gatehouse overlooking the water.

The paddle
From the car park, walk across the recreation ground to reach the riverbank. It is often muddy, so bonus points for staying dry while launching.

The first leg of the route is a quick spin up to the weir and back. Set off downstream under Albany Bridge, which carries the A244. Lavish riverside mansions with landscaped gardens line the right bank. Even the swans glide regally past Wayneflete Tower, the former gatehouse of Esher Palace. South Weylands Farm borders the river on the opposite side. Paddle up to the bridge and resist the temptation to explore the backwaters, as the estate sign sadly indicates it is private property. Check out the railway viaduct, steer clear of the weir and head back, appreciating the unobstructed waters.

Glide past the launch spot. Get ready for an adventure that is hard to believe is within the M25. With no powered boats or towpaths, this stretch offers a tranquil escape from city life. You first paddle through a residential area that reflects urban character, but the roar of traffic gently fades away. There are open meadows on the right. On the other bank is one of the UK's biggest pick-your-own farms, Garson's. If in season, parts of the route are perfumed with their lavender crops.

Follow the river upstream, winding along lush banks. Flora and fauna are plentiful. It feels like an ancient forest, with roots trailing into the water. The Mole soon narrows and it becomes more evident you are

paddling against the flow. Be ready for some obstacles, overhanging branches, patches of dense floating pennywort and even fallen trees completely blocking the way. There are surprises around every corner. How far you get depends on these obstructions. Stay safe and do not take any unnecessary risks. The combination of fallen trees and flow of the water can form strainers.

Conditions allowing, continue past Hersham Riverside Park, Woodlark Nurseries and West End Common Nature Reserve until you reach Burhill Golf Club. Getting off here is not permitted, but it is a nice spot for a picnic on the water. The return journey tests your manoeuvring skills. For added fun, see how many golf balls you can find on your way back. Ten is the number to beat.

Wildlife highlight

Banded demoiselle (*Calopteryx splendens*) Movement in the reeds? It may be the banded demoiselle, the largest species of damselfly in their favourite habitat. Along the River Mole, these delicate insects flutter in masses, their metallic blue and emerald-green bodies glinting in the sunlight. Fascinating to watch, they are among the best predators in the world, expertly catching flies, mosquitoes and aquatic insects in mid-flight. Prime time to spot them is from May to August.

> ### NEED TO KNOW
>
> ≡ No licence is required to paddle on the River Mole.
>
> ≡ Monitor river flow and water levels on the Environment Agency site or a river app. Rainfall in the Upper Mole significantly impacts the river flow in Esher. The Mole is a natural, free-flowing river, and the upstream stretch is unmanaged. It can get flashy quickly. The route is not suitable for beginners. Fallen trees and other obstructions can create strainers, even in normal conditions, requiring experience to navigate safely. In high flow, the Mole can be dangerous.
>
> ≡ A river fin may be required at lower water levels for paddleboards.
>
> ≡ Some areas are popular with anglers, be courteous and vigilant.
>
> ≡ Suitable also for canoes and kayaks.

Tuck in

Make sure to bring your own snacks, as besides Winterdown coffee trailer at the car park, there is nowhere to buy anything along the route.

LEFT Obstructions on the River Mole.

RIGHT Better to kneel through some sections.

39 WEST RESERVOIR CENTRE STOKE NEWINGTON

Discover the West Reservoir Centre, a hidden slice of nature in Zone 2. It is Hackney's best-kept secret for water lovers. From SUP to SUP yoga, kayaking, canoeing and open water swimming, this unique spot combines history, safety and tranquillity. Plan ahead, but you need to bring nothing but yourself – everything else is provided for you. With easy public transport links and on-site parking, the West Reservoir is well worth a visit.

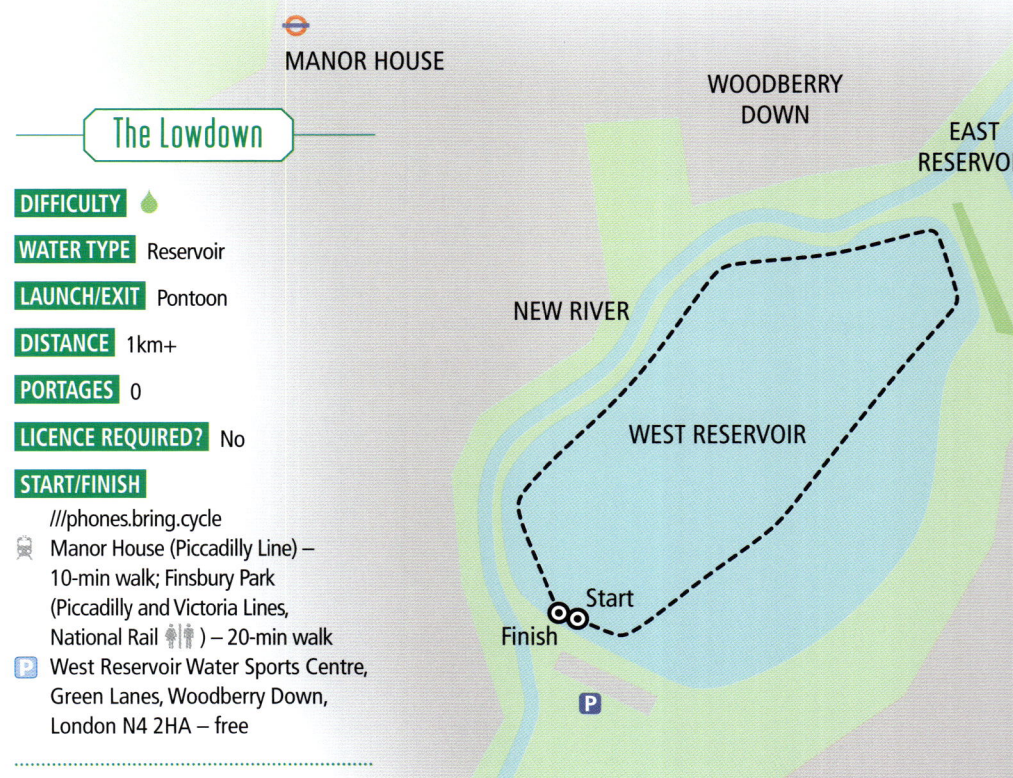

The Lowdown

DIFFICULTY

WATER TYPE Reservoir

LAUNCH/EXIT Pontoon

DISTANCE 1km+

PORTAGES 0

LICENCE REQUIRED? No

START/FINISH
///phones.bring.cycle
Manor House (Piccadilly Line) – 10-min walk; Finsbury Park (Piccadilly and Victoria Lines, National Rail) – 20-min walk
West Reservoir Water Sports Centre, Green Lanes, Woodberry Down, London N4 2HA – free

A brief history

By the 19th century, London's population and thirst was growing fast. The New River aqueduct had been supplying the capital with fresh water from Hertfordshire, but to ensure a more reliable water supply, the East and West Reservoirs were built in Stoke Newington in the 1830s, holding more than 400 million litres of water. Nine filter beds were added adjacent, a Gothic castle-style pumping station was built, and a filtration plant completed the extensive waterworks complex.

And today? The reservoirs faced development threats in the 90s, but a campaign by local residents saved them. While the filter beds were drained and built over, Hackney Council turned the West Reservoir into a watersports centre and the pumping station became an indoor climbing facility. The East Reservoir continues to function as a resource for Thames Water but doubles as Woodberry Wetlands nature reserve.

The paddle

Arrive by Tube or park at the on-site car park – the West Reservoir Centre is tucked away in between Manor House and Stoke Newington. From Green Lanes, it feels like any North London neighbourhood with terraced houses and residential blocks, local shops, a few eateries. Then, suddenly, a castle.

Impossible to miss, the fortress-like building is the old waterworks pumping station. The Victorians sure knew how to add flair to public works. Just past the castle

ABOVE The West Reservoir Centre across the water.

LEFT A quick London getaway.

is the West Reservoir Centre, a surprising expanse of water – 9 hectares within a 12-hectare site. The main building is an Art-Deco-style former filter house.

The centre's reception is on the right. To paddle, you need to have booked with Castle Canoe Club. It is members only, but do not worry, members can bring guests or you can try their £10 induction, which includes three sessions to see if membership suits you.

It is quite unreal – this large sparkling reservoir with an urban backdrop. On a warm summer's day, it feels like a holiday, so unlike London. Sailing boats line the shore, paddle craft neatly stacked in covered storage. On the water, swimming takes up the right side, a steady stream of swimmers, both leisurely and athletic, in their red caps. The left side is for watersports. Lifeguards oversee all the activities.

Enter the reservoir from the decked slipway or pontoon. The water is deep, often colder than you think. A full loop around the basin is just under a kilometre, offering plenty of room to clock in distance, practise technique or just paddle and chat with the lovely community. To the left, New River (see route 30) and a footpath run parallel, backed by modern housing developments. The top end is bordered by Woodberry Wetlands, a London Wildlife Trust reserve, and the skyline of Lincoln Court tower blocks.

Afterwards, reward yourself at the centre's waterside café or take a leisurely walk along the New River to the neighbouring nature reserve, where the café has a rooftop terrace as well. The view alone is worth it – a peaceful oasis saved by local campaigners. Next time, a swim perhaps?

Wildlife highlight

Reed warbler (*Acrocephalus scirpaceus*) Next door at Woodberry Wetlands, a mix of reed beds, hedgerows and meadows makes the perfect summer home for reed warblers after their winter in Africa. These small, plain brown birds breed from May to August, weaving their nests among the reeds. Tricky to spot, but their cheerful, chattering song gives them away every time.

OTHER WATERWAYS

LEFT Blissful SUP yoga.

BELOW Lucie Norris SUP Yoga.

RIGHT A hub for watersports lovers in Hackney.

Tuck in
The café at West Reservoir Centre and the Coal House Café at Woodberry Wetlands (free access) are both great spots.

Paddle providers
- **Castle Canoe Club** – castlecanoeclub.co.uk
- **Lucie Norris Yoga (SUP yoga)** – lucienorrisyoga.com

NEED TO KNOW

■ There is no public access to the reservoir, but paddling is offered through the Castle Canoe Club, a volunteer-run community group. The West Reservoir Centre is operated by Better and owned by Hackney Council. Membership is required, but it is affordable and all levels are welcome. Bring your own kit or use theirs. Members can paddle on Sunday mornings year-round and on Tuesday evenings in summer, with the option to bring guests for a small fee. Interested? Book ahead to try a £10 induction session, which includes two more paddles to help you decide if membership is right for you. No experience needed.

■ SUP yoga at the reservoir is available during the summer with Lucie Norris Yoga.

■ Facilities include changing rooms, toilets and an on-site café.

■ Sometimes, the water looks inky. They use dye to prevent algae growth. Water quality is tightly controlled.

40 ROYAL VICTORIA DOCK DOCKLANDS

Royal Victoria Dock is no ordinary SUP spot. The once busy dock is an unexpected coastal oasis with a sandy beach, waterfront bars, wakeboarding and open water swimming. While the sounds and sights of the industry are long gone, quayside cranes remind of the area's past. Paddle amid cable cars above you, planes from the neighbouring London City Airport and the urban jungle of Canary Wharf in the background. The enclosed waterway is perfect for beginner paddleboarders, but its scenic charm makes it a must-visit for any paddleboarder.

The Lowdown

DIFFICULTY
WATER TYPE Enclosed dock
LAUNCH/EXIT Pontoon
DISTANCE 3km+
PORTAGES 0
LICENCE REQUIRED? No
START/FINISH
 ///glory.prom.wins
 Royal Docks (cable car) – 5-min walk; Royal Victoria (DLR) – 7-min walk; Custom House (Elizabeth Line, DLR) – 15-min walk
 Check parking apps

A brief history

Royal Victoria Dock played a major role in the economic growth of London. Unlike the older docks upriver, it was purpose-built to cater to the larger steamboats. When Victoria Dock opened in 1855, it was the first enclosed dock with rail links and hydraulic lifting technology. Its success led to the construction of Royal Albert Dock in 1880, to the east of Victoria Dock. Together, these docks became London's main hub for handling various commodities. The King George V Dock followed in 1921, and the combined Royal Docks became the largest body of enclosed docks in the world.

Sadly, the docks were severely damaged by wartime bombing and struggled to adapt to containerised cargo. Their eventual closure in 1980 led to high levels of deprivation in the area. Today, the Royal Docks are on a new chapter of regeneration as an Enterprise Zone.

The paddle

ABOVE A windy day at Wakeup Docklands and feeling very small.

Public transport links to the Royal Victoria Dock, the largest of three docks in the Royal Docks of East London, are excellent. Arrive by the DLR, Elizabeth Line or, for a more dramatic entrance, opt for the cable car. Walk to the WakeUp Docklands' hut in the south-western corner of the dock and check in for your pre-booked session at reception. After the on-land formalities, you are good to go and explore the enclosed body of water.

An inlet of the River Thames, the length of the water area is about 1.5km, width 200m. Because of its history as a commercial dock, the water is deep, averaging at 8m, but as deep as 13m at points. Due to the depth, the water may be colder than you think. Regular safety tests are carried out to ensure water quality.

Mind the wakeboarders and open water swimmers on your left and head towards London City Airport, following the southern bank. It is peaceful on the water, but due to the vast expanse of open water, it is susceptible to wind and chop.

You can imagine the busy dock days when paddling next to the 14 quayside cranes along the banks. The Royal Victoria Dock Footbridge connects Custom House and Silvertown, creating a wind tunnel. Further east looms the derelict Spillers Millennium Mills, undergoing major renovation as part of Silvertown redevelopment. If access is

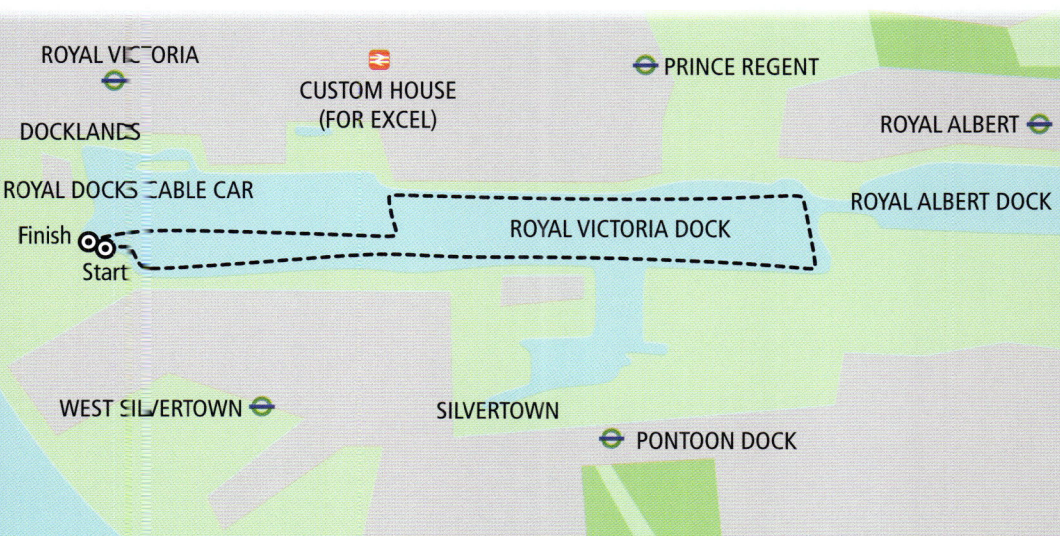

ABOVE Sculpture dedicated to dock workers at Custom House.

BELOW A wide view of Royal Victoria Dock.

floating hotel, the Sunborn, from a new perspective. The Good Hotel is another on-the-water hotel. It is hard to believe that it is a former Dutch floating prison, towed here across the North Sea.

The return journey opens up a view of cable cars gliding over the River Thames, connecting Greenwich Peninsula to the Royal Docks, with the striking skyline of Canary Wharf and the distinctive dome of the O2 in the distance – a scene that is hard to beat.

Wildlife highlight

Feral pigeon (*Columba livia domestica*) The feral pigeon, a descendant of the rock dove, is one of London's most common birds. They have swapped rocky shores for city skylines, nesting among buildings and cranes at Royal Victoria Dock, where food, water and shelter are plentiful. Ever wondered why you never see baby pigeons? Their chicks, called squabs, stay in the nest until nearly full-grown. And pigeons are loyal, and mate for life. They don't mind that they are often seen as pests, as whether perched in an alley or on a fancy rooftop, they strut through London as if they own the place.

still available, take a spin in Pontoon Dock. All the way at the bottom is Silo D. James Bond fans may recognise the scenery from 'The World Is Not Enough'.

Back in the main inlet on the north bank, admire the Excel Centre and a luxury

OTHER WATERWAYS 203

ABOVE Taking it all in.

NEED TO KNOW

■ There is no public right of access to the docks. The Royal Docks Management Authority oversee the water areas. Access for paddleboarding is exclusively through WakeUp Docklands. A small launch fee applies and BSUPA 'Ready to Ride' or equivalent certification of proficiency is required, adults only. Buoyancy aids and leashes are compulsory. Book in advance on their website; season is usually April–October.

■ No kayaking or canoeing.

Tuck in

After your SUP session, relax with a drink at WakeUp Docklands' beach bar or the Oiler Bar next door. On sunny days, it feels like being transported to an exotic holiday destination. If you brought your own snacks, enjoy them on the dockside or in the City Hall garden. There are also several places to eat and drink on the northern bank. For the finest view, head to the Good Hotel rooftop terrace (open to all).

Paddle provider
WakeUp Docklands – wakeupdocklands.com

BEYOND THE PADDLE

Paddling London's waterways has deepened my connection to the city's green and blue spaces. I notice more, care more and want to understand more. Luckily, there are endless opportunities to feed this passion. In case this happens to you, here are some of my off-the-water favourites:

Places

Crossness Pumping Station: take a guided tour of the ornate Victorian sewage works – crossness.org.uk

London Canal Museum: learn about London's canal history in Islington – canalmuseum.org.uk

London Museum Docklands (free): discover London's maritime past in Canary Wharf – londonmuseum.org.uk

London Museum of Water & Steam: understand the city's water story in Brentford – waterandsteam.org.uk

Thames Barrier: visit London's flood defence near Woolwich – gov.uk/guidance/the-thames-barrier

Totally Thames Festival: celebrate arts and culture every September on, beneath or along the river – thamesfestivaltrust.org

Tower Bridge: the Behind-the-Scenes Tour runs in winter only and must be booked in advance as it often sells out – towerbridge.org.uk.

Tate Britain has a collection of JMW Turner's river-inspired paintings and London often hosts exceptional art events, like the Monet and London, Views of the Thames exhibition at the Courtauld in 2025.

Conservation

London Wildlife Trust – wildlondon.org.uk

Thames Estuary Partnership – thamesestuarypartnership.org

Thames21 – thames21.org.uk

Podcasts

CanalCast by the Canal & River Trust offers a behind-the-scenes look at how they care for 2,000 miles of canals and rivers, from wildlife to waterway maintenance. After a few episodes, I didn't mind paying my licence fees at all.

Talk of the Thames by the Thames Estuary Partnership explores the tidal Thames – its history, wildlife, riverside changes, environmental challenges and the people who work on or enjoy the river.

Books

How to Read Water – Tristan Gooley

Local: A Search for Nearby Nature and Wildness – Alastair Humphreys

London's Docklands, an Illustrated History – Geoff Marshall

London's Lost Rivers – Paul Talling

Londonist Mapped: Hand-drawn Maps for the Urban Explorer (Londonist)

Nicholson Waterways Guide 1: Grand Union, Oxford & the South East (Collins)

Nicholson Waterways Guide 7: River Thames & the Southern Waterways (Collins)

Paddle the Thames – Mark Rainsley

Pub Paddles – Peter Knowles

Stand-up Paddleboarding in Great Britain – Jo Moseley

Thames, Sacred River – Peter Ackroyd

Water Ways: A Thousand Miles Along Britain's Canals – Jasper Winn

Maps

Grand Union Canal – Milton Keynes to London, with the London and East London Rings (Heron Maps)

Lee and Stort Navigations, with East London Ring and the Bow Back Rivers (Heron Maps)

River Thames and the Thames Path (Heron Maps)

Online resources

Citymapper (citymapper.com) – My favourite travel app for getting around town. It shows all modes of urban transport with live timings, important when there are disruptions or engineering works.

CanalPlanAC (canalplan.uk) – A handy planner for inland waterway journeys, especially if you want more detailed info, lock by lock.

Go Paddling (gopaddling.info) – Paddle UK's go-to site for leisure paddling. Find routes, safety advice and local clubs all in one place.

OS Maps (osmaps.com) – Perfect for paddle mapping. Browse routes made by others or map out your own.

Paddle UK (paddleuk.org.uk) – The national body for paddle sports in the UK. Whether you're racing, getting qualified or just paddling for fun, this is the place to start. And to get your on-the-water membership.

SUPjunkie (supjunkie.co.uk) – The place to find SUP events and races in the UK and beyond, with live coverage, videos and interviews.

More to explore

This book is part of a growing shelf of paddle guides published by Adlard Coles, Bloomsbury. If you've enjoyed this title, there are plenty more:

Great British Paddling Adventures – Richard Harpham & Ashley Kenlock

Paddle and Pub – Gemma Bowes

Paddle Scotland – Alasdair Findlay

Paddle the East of England – Jess Ashley, Oli Jordan, Andy Large and Matt Payne

The Paddleboard Bible – Dave Price

Paddling in London led me to writing this book.
                    Who knows where it may take you?

ACKNOWLEDGEMENTS

Writing *Paddle London* came about through a series of coincidences and the generosity of many people. Thank you to Jo Moseley for championing me as the go-to London paddle writer. I'm grateful to Bloomsbury Publishing and my commissioning editor, Clara Jump, for believing in the wider appeal of a London paddle guide.

I had no idea how much expertise went into turning raw material into a book. My thanks to project editor Harriet Newcombe, copyeditor Jenni Davis, cartographer Richard Thomson, designer Rod Teasdale and the extended Bloomsbury team for bringing it all together.

This book is a mix of my own paddle experiences and research. I'm grateful to everyone who paddled with me, shared knowledge or offered support. Special thanks to friends who joined me on the water – Louise Nolan, Jessica Light, Izzy Cortez-Gomes, Sarah Thornely, Sam Miyano Pitt, Claire Billard, Charles Hayden, Samantha Coleman, Ansa Celestine, Tonya Babb, Carol Luck, Meghan Takwani, Melissande Box, Tilda Senaris, Jill Nicholson, Kate Swanson, Sari Wildsmith, Mary Newell-Price, Margaret Hulse, Judith Schmid, Hester Hearn, Shilpa Rasaiah, Nicola Baird, Isabelle Leduc, Rob Meade, Tara and Phil Crist, Diana Thorne and Vicky Phillips – for your company and for patiently waiting while I stopped for photos.

Thanks also to the clubs I paddled with: Active360, Blue Chip SUPer Club, Dittons Paddle Boarding, London SUP Squad, LSUPCO, Paddleboard Maidenhead, Paddleboarding London and SUP at Islington.

Finally, to my partner Fabienne Segarra. You made it possible for me to write, taking care of everything while I sat with my laptop. Thank you for being amazing and for enduring another one of my crazy projects.

PHOTO CREDITS

All photos are the author's unless otherwise stated:

James Brennan / The London Stand Up Paddle Co (pp. 69 bottom, 72 top and bottom, 77), **Paul Hyman / Active360** (p. 87 top), **Louise Nolan** (p. 100 bottom), **Lucie Norris Yoga** (pp. 198, 199 bottom), **Paddle Up Ltd** (p. 65 top), **Brett Scillitoe / AquaPaddle** (pp. 48-9 bottom, 53), **Fabienne Segarra** (half-title page, pp. 15, 97, 118 top and bottom, 119 bottom, 139, 146, 147, 172 top and bottom, 201, 202 top, 203 top), **Rod Teasdale** (pp. 94, 95), **Sarah Thornely / SUPjunkie** (p. 59), **Harry Whelan / London Kayak Company** (pp. 90, 91, 92, 93), **Andrew Wyborn / Hampton Court Paddle Sports** (p. 51).

Huge thanks to those who have shared their pictures – so grateful.

INDEX

B
Basingstoke Canal 176–83
Battersea to Greenwich 89–95
Brent, River 115–19
Brentford to Fox Inn at Hanwell 115–19
Broxbourne
　Hertford to 158–61
　to Ponders End 162–5
buoyancy aids/PFDs 11, 12

C
Camden
　to King's Cross 138–41
　to Maida Hill Tunnel 133–7
canals 96–7
　Basingstoke 176–83
　Grand Union 98–132
　Lee Navigation 150–73
　Regents 133–49
Chelsea to Kew 84–8
Clapton to Hackney Wick 170–3
clothing 11, 12
Colt Hill
　Crookham Wharf to 176–9
　to Greywell Tunnel 180–3
Crookham Wharf to Colt Hill 176–9

D
Docklands 200–3
dry bags/packing for trip 14

E
ebb tide flag warning system, River Thames 19
Eel Pie Island, Richmond to 71–4
Ember, River, Thames Ditton to 52–7
equipment 11, 12
Esher to Hersham 193–5

F
food and drink 11

G
Godalming to Shepperton 184–8
Grand Union Canal 98–132
Greenford
　to Harlesden 124–7
　Hayes to 120–3
Greenwich, Battersea to 89–95
Greywell Tunnel, Colt Hill to 180–3

H
Hackney
　Islington to 142–5
　to Mile End 146–9
Hackney Wick, Clapton to 170–3
Ham House to Teddington Lock 67–70
Hampton Court
　Kingston to 58–62
　Windsor to 34–9
Hampton to Molesey and Thames Aits 46–51
Hanwell
　Brentford to Fox Inn at 115–19
　Hayes to 110–14

Harlesden, Greenford to 124–7
Hayes
　to Greenford 120–3
　to Hanwell 110–14
Hedsor Water, Maidenhead to 26–9
Hersham, Esher to 193–5
Hertford to Broxbourne 158–61

I
Islington to Hackney 142–5

J
Jubilee River 189–92

K
Kensal Green, Little Venice to 128–32
Kew Bridge
　Putney to 80–3
　to Richmond 75–9
Kew, Chelsea to 84–8
King's Cross, Camden to 138–41
Kingston
　to Hampton Court 58–62
　to Teddington 63–6

L
leashes, SUP 11, 12
Lee Navigation 150–73
Limehouse Basin 150–3
Limehouse Loop 154–7
Little Venice to Kensal Green 128–32
London Legacy Loop 150–3

INDEX CONTINUED

M
Maida Hill Tunnel, Camden to 133–7
Maidenhead to Hedsor Water 26–9
Manor Farm, Marsh Lane to 189–92
Marsh Lane to Manor Farm 189–92
Mile End, Hackney to 146–9
Mole, River 193–5
Molesey and Thames Aits, Hampton to 46–51

N
navigation 14

P
Paddle UK SUP safety guidelines 10–11
phones 11
planning 10–11
Ponders End
 Broxbourne to 162–5
 to Tottenham Hale 166–9
Putney Bridge 18
Putney to Kew Bridge 80–3

R
Reading to Wargrave via St Patrick's Stream 20–5
Regent's Canal 133–49
responsible paddling 14
Richmond
 to Eel Pie Island 71–4
 Ham House to Teddington Lock 67–70
 Kew Bridge to 75–9
Richmond Lock & Weir 19
Rickmansworth
 to Uxbridge 102–5
 to Watford 98–101
Royal Victoria Dock 200–3
rules, waterway 11

S
safety 10–15
Saint Patrick's Stream 24, 25
Shepperton, Godalming to 184–8
Slough, West Drayton to 106–9
Stoke Newington 196–9

T
Teddington Lock 17
 Ham House to 67–70
Thames Barrier 19
Thames Ditton to River Ember 52–7
Thames, River 16–17, 20–95
 ebb tide flag warning system 19
 non-tidal Thames 18
 river flow rate 17–18
 tidal Thames 18–19
tides
 see Thames, River
Tideway Code, PLA 18
toilets 14
Tottenham Hale, Ponders End to 166–9
traffic, river 16, 18

U
Uxbridge, Rickmansworth to 102–5

W
Wargrave via St Patrick's Stream, Reading to 20–5
water quality 14
Watford, Rickmansworth to 98–101
weather forecasts 10–11
West Drayton to Slough 106–9
West Reservoir Centre 196–9
Wey Navigations 184–8
Weybridge 40–5
Windsor
 and Backwaters 30–3
 to Hampton Court 34–9
winter paddling 14